MOSQUITO
TO
BERLIN

MOSQUITO
TO
BERLIN

*The Story of Ed 'Bertie' Boulter, DFC,
One of Bennett's Pathfinders*

by

Peter Bodle FRAeS
and
Bertie Boulter DFC

Pen & Sword
AVIATION

First published in Great Britain in 2007 by
Pen & Sword Aviation
an imprint of
Pen & Sword Books Ltd

ISBN 978-1-84415-488-3

British Library Cataloguing-in-Publication Data
A CIP catalogue record for this book is
available from the British Library

Typeset in Palatino by
Phoenix Typesetting, Auldgirth, Dumfriesshire

Printed and bound in England by
Biddles Ltd, King's Lynn

Pen & Sword Books Ltd incorporates the Imprints of Pen & Sword Aviation,
Pen & Sword Maritime, Pen & Sword Military, Wharncliffe Local History,
Pen & Sword Select, Pen & Sword Military Classics and Leo Cooper.

For a complete list of Pen & Sword titles please contact
PEN & SWORD BOOKS LIMITED
47 Church Street, Barnsley, South Yorkshire, S70 2AS, England
E-mail: enquiries@pen-and-sword.co.uk
Website: www.pen-and-sword.co.uk

To Christine
and
all my colleagues who flew and served with me.

The Flying Field

Then! But now,
green changed to gold;
furrowed by the plough
We, who remain grow old.

Bombers' prayers,
disguised with laughter,
hid their cares–
Thereafter.

Merlin's voice, no more
from dusk to dawn.
Its silent roar
is cradled in the corn.

Wings once soared high
among forgotten years;
Yet loved ones waved goodbye
and we have shed our tears.

R.H.M. Vere, 1409 Met Flight.

Contents

	Introduction	ix
1	From Norwich to Theodore and Back	1
2	Pilot Training	7
3	Back to England	27
4	Blenheims and Mosquitos	41
5	First Operations	54
6	November 1944	62
7	December 1944	81
8	January 1945	89
9	February 1945	99
10	March 1945	105
11	April 1945	114
12	The last Operation and Beyond	121
13	Flying For Fun	138
	Appendix 1 Aircraft Flown	152
	Appendix 2 Operations Flown	154
	Appendix 3 The Pathfinders	157
	Bibliography	159
	Index	161

Introduction

When Air Vice Marshal Don Bennett originally formed the Pathfinder Squadrons in the autumn of 1942, many of the pilots chosen to fly these lead 'marker' operations for Bomber Command were veteran pilots with a wealth of experience to see them through. Many, however, were not. Many were in fact young men with no combat experience whatsoever; some were not even out of their teens, and some were Commonwealth citizens far from their native lands. I was one of these young men and I qualified on all three counts.

My parents christened me Herbert Edward and I was called Eddie. When I joined 128 Squadron Ivor Broom renamed me Bertie. That was the name I answered to from then on. For the sake of continuity that is the name I have used throughout this book.

Like so many of my contemporaries, my one aim in life was to become a pilot and to have a go at the enemy. By the time I was eighteen and old enough to volunteer, be trained and gain enough experience to face the enemy, World War II had already gone through several phases. The Battle of Britain, with its emphasis on the skills and courage of the Spitfire and Hurricane pilots, who were heroes to us all, was a year or more into history. At that time the efforts of Bomber Command were stalling, as the planes and equipment at their disposal were not accurate enough to have the desired effect and the losses being suffered were unacceptable and unsustainable. It was now time for the pilots and navigators of the smaller, lighter Pathfinder bombers, the ultra-fast de Havilland Mosquitos to step forward and make their mark. I was lucky enough to be chosen as one of those pilots.

Twice the fortunes of war caused me to evacuate my aircraft in mid-air, both times with more or less successful results. Several times mechanical failure caused me to jettison the bomb load and abort the operation for that night, but every time I was fortunately able to return to the fray with unquenched determination and resolve. I was blessed with a great squadron commander in Ivor Broom, a stalwart room mate and friend in Tommy Broom and three superb navigators, Jim Churcher, Chris Hart and Derek Spinks. Jim and Chris guided me through all my bombing operations from start to finish including nineteen to Berlin, and Derek navigated and flew all round Europe with me immediately after the war until I finally left the service to pursue a career in industry.

More than fifty years on I was fortunate enough still to be flying the Stearman in which I had originally gained my wings, and to meet regularly with the survivors of the Pathfinder squadrons, including Ivor and Tommy Broom. It is these memories I share with you, and to these life-long comrades that I dedicate this book.

Eddie 'Bertie' Boulter DFC

CHAPTER ONE

From Norwich to Theodore and Back

In the early twentieth century the idea of serving one's country was a family tradition passed on as if by instinct from father to son in the Boulter family, as well as being firmly ingrained in the character of most of the Canadian citizens of the day. Having emigrated from Norwich in 1909, Herbert Claude Boulter settled in Theodore, Saskatchewan, a small but growing agricultural community deep in the central plains of southern Canada. There he worked as a farm labourer on various local farms for five years. Later, as the drums of war beat over Europe, as an ex-Territorial Army volunteer, he heard the call early and enlisted in the Canadian Army. Soon, after just a few months of induction and training, he found himself once again back in his native England. From there he went to war. He served mainly in France with the Canadian Army Service Corps as a horseman in the transportation section, carting shells and other munitions to the front lines. Amazingly for a war epitomized by the carnage of troops at or near the front line he survived physically intact, but as with so many others the war took its toll in other ways.

When he was demobbed in late 1918 he returned to Theodore with his new English bride. She was a Norwich girl, Annie Eliza (known as Trixie), a young lady for whom he had gone AWOL on at least two occasions during the previous

1

couple of years, much to the anger of his immediate superiors. Surprisingly, he seemed to have got away with it, for it was not unknown for soldiers going AWOL to be classified as deserters and to be put in front of a court martial, and perhaps even a firing squad. To have got away with it twice, attracting just a fine on each occasion, bordered on the miraculous. But the Canadian officer corps that he served under was known to be more humane than its British counterpart.

Five years later Claude and Trixie's only child was born. On 15 April 1923 Herbert Edward Boulter, weighed in at 7½ pounds to swell Theodore's modest but growing population. He was a normal, healthy child brought up in a rural farming community. Even so by the time he was four or five it was obvious to his parents that he was never going to be 6 feet tall or have the physique to star in the Theodore Wildcats ice hockey team. This slightness of stature would, however, serve him well some twenty or so years later when scrambling rather hurriedly in and out of various combat aircraft became a regular part of his life.

When he was five his father bought a Shetland pony named Peggy and a two-wheeled cart. Some of his earliest memories were of this pony and treks with his father in the Whitesands River area as he carted goods from Theodore to the outlying farms and settlements. Soon after this came the advent of the Model T and Model A Ford trucks, the latter of which was put to work carting gravel and aggregate to the construction sites of the new Highway 14.

At the age of seven he first entered the portals of Theodore School on Main Street and came under the watchful eyes of teachers Jean Walker and Ivy Tindale, and the supervision of the school principal Mr Preston Pollock. Theodore School was the only brick building in the area. It had four classrooms, two on the ground floor and two on the first floor, while the basement housed the toilets, the cloakrooms and the very efficient central-heating system.

Bertie's school years were happy ones. Jean Walker and Ivy

Tindale were both caring and dedicated teachers. The principal was a kindly but ailing man who was replaced in Bertie's latter years at the school by Pat Schmidt and Edwin Conrad. As principal Conrad was both a gentleman and a devoted educationalist, who would frequently give extra after-hours coaching to any pupil who was struggling. Often in the early evening Bertie or some of his fellow classmates would return to school for extra help in the subjects causing them difficulties; all this at a time when the great depression was causing social deprivation generally, including the necessity for the Theodore teachers' wages to be cut quite severely. None of this changed Conrad's beliefs in his role in education and his need to do the best by his pupils.

> Life was never boring. There were many 'after school' activities including school plays and camping expeditions on the shores of Devils Lake, where we met the kids from other villages. Music was a strong interest all year round, either playing instruments with friends and other Theodore pupils or listening to it at home on the battery-powered radio in a corner of the sitting room. During the winter we had both a curling rink and a skating rink to entertain us. Life for schoolchildren in Saskatchewan was good, we were proud to be Canadian and proud to be a part of England and King George.
> Life at home was also good as my mother made cheese from the milk of our own cow and cured ham and bacon, and of course baked her own bread. There was usually milk left over which got given to neighbours who in turn usually had something extra from their own store that they would exchange in return. My father occasionally brought home some fresh water fish to make a good wholesome diet for us all.

On 14 February 1937 life changed dramatically when Bertie's father died at the very young age of fifty-two. He suffered a severe stroke, probably as a combination of long hours of very hard work and an uncommon liking for locally brewed Ukrainian vodka. The Mercer boys, Harald and Richard, and their family were a great help to Bertie and his mother at that time. Schooling continued and their life went on as best it could. Soon after his father's funeral, however, his mother decided to return home, although it took a while to organize. Apart from anything else, the young Bertie was Canadian and he had no particular desire to go to England, or to leave his friends. Eighteen months later Trixie Boulter brought her teenage son to England and back to her roots in Norwich.

> In early December 1938 we boarded the train to Winnipeg, where we stopped overnight while we waited for the train to Montreal. Coming from Theodore, Winnipeg seemed enormous. I doubted my mother's word that Montreal was even bigger. I simply could not believe anywhere could be bigger than Winnipeg. I also could not understand why there was no one there who I knew. After all, in Theodore I knew everyone.

The Boulters moved in with Bertie's Aunt Gladys, her husband Jerry Mather and their daughter Gwen, at 52 Grant Street, just off the Dereham Road in Norwich. Within days of arriving, Bertie had secured a job with the engineering company Barnards on Mouseold Heath as an office junior. In fact he spent most of his first few weeks in the same office as the wages clerk. Within a week or so he was assigned the job of clock-card clerk, under the watchful gaze of the wages clerk Reggie Temple, calculating the wages for the firm's workforce from their weekly clock cards and the company rates of pay; all this for the princely sum of 7s 6d a week.
This new life was not easy for a young Canadian confronted with the broad Norfolk dialect and the quaint British pounds, shillings and pence, rather than the dollar and cent system that he had used all his life. He also took a while to get used to the English road system, where all roads radiated from the

city centre. It was most confusing for a prairie boy and he frequently got lost riding his borrowed bicycle to and from work. The next three months saw him move to the progress office, where he was overseen by Herbert Buxton, a thorough but rather pedantic character who instilled in the young Bertie the need for attention to detail.

Six months later he finally put all this office work behind him as he was moved across the works to the engineering plant itself and made responsible for commissioning the long defunct anodizing plant that was languishing under a thick layer of dust and cobwebs in a dark, forgotten corner of the works. Because the country had only recently started to climb out from the great depression, Barnards, like so many other flourishing companies, was awash with very good and experienced men, all capable of far more but grateful to have a job of any sort. This was an ideal learning environment for a young, lively enquiring mind. Bertie was teamed up with one of the works inspectors, a Mr Page. He learned a lot, and quickly. Soon there was a large and profitable volume of war work, anodizing selections of aircraft parts which flowed constantly through the factory. One of the first jobs tackled by the Page / Boulter team, once the plant was fully operational, was to anodize sections of aircraft bomb racks manufactured at the Boulton & Paul factory, just a few minutes down the road from the Barnards site.

Shortly after the plant became fully productive, Bertie's training and experience were further enhanced as his skills on the equipment in the machine shop were perfected – to the extent that he was moved across to the capstan lathe section, promoted to setter and put in charge of six machines and their female operators. These were local ladies with no industrial, workplace or engineering background whatsoever. They were all good workers, but totally inexperienced. Amazingly the team became successful, despite this inexperience and having a 17-year-old Canadian country boy in charge. Bertie himself had received no formal engineering training whatsoever, just a couple of years of hands-on experience and one night a week at Norwich Technical School. His acquisition of people skills, with a team of ladies to look after as well as providing their technical support, was equally rapid.

He also learned a few military disciplines and he joined Barnards' platoon of the Home Guard, where he was equipped with a Springfield rifle that was almost as long as he was tall. He was also assigned guard duty as a Lewis machine gunner during the day when the *Luftwaffe* sent in Heinkel 111s and Dornier JU88s on hit-and-run bombing raids over Norwich.

Tuesday, 15 April 1941 saw Bertie's eighteenth birthday. He took the morning off and presented himself at the recruitment office in Norwich. Once provisionally accepted, all he had to do was explain to his foreman Joe Latus, why he had not been at work that morning. Joe was from the old school and took absenteeism as seriously as any military officer, as he explained to Bertie when he finally put in an appearance. It was only when he explained that he had decided to leave the relative comfort and security of a reserved occupation and volunteer for aircrew that the foreman's severity softened. Bertie already knew that Joe's own son, Jack had done exactly the same thing himself only a few weeks earlier.

It took quite a few weeks for the papers and travel warrants to find their way to Grant Street, so Bertie settled down to acquire and develop a few more engineering skills from the tradesmen in the engineering shop, skills that would serve him well several decades later when he owned his own company. In the meantime, there was a war to fight.

CHAPTER TWO

Pilot Training

T he long-awaited buff envelope containing travel documents and Bertie's official invitation to join His Majesty's armed forces arrived in early August. He had earlier been instructed to attend a medical centre in London for assessment, where he had been prodded, poked and injected, before being declared fighting fit. He was then sent to the local dentist in Norwich to have an oral examination and the fillings deemed necessary before he could enter basic training.

He was instructed to present himself at Lord's cricket ground on 18 August, as were hundreds of other would-be pilots and aircrew. Several young and eager hopefuls from the local area met up on the platform at Norwich station and travelled down to London together. In the same compartment for the 2½ hour journey were Don Plumb, who worked in a solicitor's office, another local lad named Tony Platten, who appeared to be more sophisticated than the rest of them and seemed to consider himself potential officer material. The 'old man' of the group, was Joe Beckett, who was all of twenty-four years old, already married with two children. The underground took them the eight stops from Liverpool Street station to St John's Wood. The short walk through the war-torn London streets to Lord's was a real eye opener to him; he had no real experience of big city life, never mind one of the world's major capitals.

An extremely impressive selection of gold-braided caps

greeted the recruits when they got to Lord's. They were treated to a well-rehearsed and no doubt often repeated pep talk, but it worked. They all felt totally overawed, almost as if they were in the presence of gods. Bertie glanced to his left and then to his right and noticed that the row of braid seemed to stretch well into the distance in both directions behind the long row of bare wooden tables. When the pep talk finished they were organized into groups and sent to accommodation billets in Abbey Road, St John's Wood. It would be their home for the next six weeks as they undertook their induction training, it felt more like six months.

In Abbey Road, several apartment blocks had been requisitioned by the War Ministry and converted to barrack blocks with four of us recruits to each room, including the living room. Sleeping in two-tier bunks twenty to twenty-four chaps could be housed in one apartment. For me this was another new experience, not having any brothers or sisters had obviously meant my room had always been my own. Not any more; suddenly I was part of a team. For this team though the team leaders were something quite different, they were all RAF corporal PT instructors. I had never come across people like this before. All the new recruits were convinced that they were soldiers who had been expelled from the German SS for excessive behaviour. They drilled us; they taught us to march (well nearly all of us), they took us on runs and they put us through exercises . . . all day and every day. Knees, ankles and calf muscles suffered greatly; most of my fellow recruits were all terribly unfit specimens.

Even the journey to have our meals at Regent's Park Zoo was a full-blown exercise. Some of the intake were tall, long-legged ex-policemen, and as such had some experience of marching. Thus they were put in the lead of the squad as we marched along the London streets.

This meant those raw recruits in the middle of the squad were trotting to keep up and the unfortunates at the rear, including me, were frequently to be seen running. The squad stopped for no one, least of all a tired A/C2 [Aircraftsman Second Class], the lowest form of human life in the RAF.

The food was at best unappetizing, at worst almost inedible. No doubt the RAF worked on the theory that hungry teenagers will eat anything, and for six weeks they did. Standard meals usually comprised meat, potatoes and cabbage, followed by pie and custard. The meat was inevitably tough, the vegetables overcooked and the gravy thin and tasteless. It could also be cold if you arrived late. It was served by dozens of recruits who looked as unhappy as the diners. They were surly and uninterested, and seemed to have less interest in what they were doing than Bertie and his fellows did in their basic training.

The recruits sat on long benches and ate off trestle tables and benches in rows of hundreds. Cutlery was always cold and wet from being rinsed through from the previous sitting. Bertie never once had a meal with a dry knife or fork for the whole six weeks. It was simply a matter of feeding a never-ending production line of hungry recruits.

If he and his colleagues had only basic facilities for their meals, then their next medical examination was a real eye opener, certainly for any onlookers. With no other facilities available, their 'below waist' medical inspection at St John's Wood was held with trousers down and shirt up outside in the street. There was no false modesty allowed in the wartime RAF! The medical officer (MO) had a swagger stick he used to prod, poke or lift and move body parts he wished to see more clearly. Clearly it was a very hygienic system for him.

From 18 August to 9 September time dragged. About this time the uniforms started to arrive – piecemeal. By the third week of training they were still looking a motley crew, some with jackets and no issue trousers, some with trousers and no issue shirts. It took most of the six weeks of basic training to kit them all out completely.

Then by a strange quirk of fate it was back to Norfolk. Along with some of his Abbey Road colleagues, he was sent to Initial Training Wing (ITW) Bircham-Newton, a remote airfield in the north-west of the county, fairly close to the royal estate of Sandringham. They were billeted nearby in the servants' quarters at Ken Hill House, the family seat of Sir Lycett Green, just a mile or two down the road from the seaside village of Snettisham. There were about fifty or so of the young RAF recruits housed there under the command of Flying Officer (F/O) Armitage. As the commanding officer (C/O) of Bircham ITW, Armitage had a sergeant and three corporal instructors to assist him in the task of turning these very raw recruits into something approaching a team of airmen that could be of use to the RAF. Armitage took basic navigation and Air Force law, while Sergeant Penfold, who was a bit of a father figure to Bertie and his colleagues as he was at least thirty years old, handled administration and discipline. He was particularly keen to instil in all his young charges how imperative it was never to call any RAF officer a bastard, however much they deserved it – although out of earshot he considered it was all right. One of the corporal instructors took charge of keeping them all fit. Nonetheless, compared to Abbey Road, this was heaven. The food was good, they were 'proper airmen' at last and learning some-thing they felt was worthwhile, and to cap it all by the end of the course they became leading aircraftsmen (LAC) with a propeller badge to sew on their sleeves to prove it. They still had the white flash in their caps as trainees and would keep them for at least the next twelve months, but they had taken the first step up the ladder towards being a pilot. All this in about three months.

Aircrew Dispersal Centre (ACDC) Brighton was their next home for a couple of weeks until their real training in real aeroplanes could begin. There the rather splendid seafront hotels, the Grand and the Metropole, were used as billets and the horrors of Abbey Road were soon pushed to the back of their minds.

By 15 December, just as the cold and damp of winter were setting in, Pilot Officer (P/O) Watson, attached to No. 18 Elementary Flying Training School (EFTS) at Fairoaks in Surrey, helped Bertie complete that final step towards getting airborne. For thirty-five minutes on a cold, grey, misty winter day he took him through his first faltering steps of pilot training in D.H. Tiger Moth T6050. Like so many *ab initio* pilots of the day, they went through an air-experience check, a study of the cockpit layout, the exercise covering the effects of controls and their first efforts of flying an aeroplane straight and level. Forty minutes after take-off he was back on the ground making his way back to the school buildings. The talk amongst the cadets for the remainder of the day was of nothing else. For once even the food came second on their agenda.

The following morning he and P/O Watson clambered aboard Tiger Moth T7347 and spent a further fifty-five minutes practising flying straight and level and conducting a practical demonstration on the effects of the controls. As it was a somewhat longer sortie than the first, lesson 5 from the manual was added, and climbing, gliding and spinning were included in the day's activities. Also on that day all students were initiated into the delicate art of taxiing a Tiger Moth – not a simple task for the inexperienced novice and a procedure alive with pitfalls to trap the unwary and the slow of thinking. All these feats were added to the list of accomplishments later entered in the green-covered Form 414, the RAF pilot's flying log-book issued to LAC Boulter H.E. 1388911.

Later that same afternoon the Boulter/Watson team paired up again and spent an additional thirty minutes in T7347 further perfecting lessons 4 (flying straight and level) and 5, (climbing, gliding and stalling). By now the weather had improved very slightly and the instructions yelled by P/O Watson through the Tiger Moth's speaking system (known as the Gosport tube) were starting to make a bit more sense. The following day lessons 6 (medium turns) and 10 (spinning) were demonstrated and practised for forty minutes, along with further work on lessons 4 and 5.

A change of both instructor and aircraft came on 18 December as the previous skills were practised again for forty-five minutes under the watchful eye of Sergeant (Sgt) Graesser in Tiger Moth T6800. Taking off into wind (lesson 7) was also added to the curriculum. The erratic attempts at taxiing were by now starting to become less dramatic and instructor intervention was becoming less frequent. There was then a four-day break until 22 December, when it was back to the familiarity of P/O Watson and T7347 to cover more of the same for three-quarters of an hour, plus a progression to lesson 9 that introduced Bertie to the art of glide approaches and landing. The sortie on Christmas Eve was spent honing the skills of taking off into wind and more practice at the glide approach and landing. When it was over almost another hour was entered in the 2nd Pilot, Pupil or Passenger section of his logbook.

The briefest of breaks to celebrate the Christmas festivities ended on the morning after Boxing Day. Although Bertie had been unable to get home for Christmas (the first one he had ever spent away from his family), he and another cadet enjoyed Boxing Day with a family in Woking and tucked into a good civilian lunch followed by a brisk afternoon walk with their hosts and their dogs. On 27 December a further thirty minutes flying circuits with Sgt Graesser in N9455, brought the Boulter log book entry up to the heady total of five hours and thirty-five minutes. Sgt Graesser was the instructor again on both that day and the next, when a further forty and twenty-five minutes respectively were added, to bring the grand total flying hours to six hours, forty minutes. It all seemed to have happened so quickly. It was, however, enough for the Assistant Chief Instructor of No. 18 EFTS, Squadron Leader Cubitt, who duly stamped the next page under Sgt Graesser's signature and countersigned the entry as sufficient experience for Boulter H.E. 1388911 to go forward for pilot training. It was 3 January 1942.

A second ACDC followed at a snowy Heaton Park, Manchester. Again this was a short-term stay as they awaited their transport across the Atlantic where they were to commence their aircrew training courses. At Heaton Park they were billeted out in homes in the local area. Bertie and one of his colleagues shared a room in the home of a local family, where they were very well looked after, although the weather made it a less than enjoyable stay. Even a walk into Manchester to see the film *White Christmas* failed to cheer them very much.

On 23 January they were on their travels again, this time to the Scottish port of Gourock in the Firth of Clyde. There they met up with a troopship that was destined to take them in an escorted convoy to America. As they set sail the next day the weather was foul, and within a few hours it deteriorated even further. By the time they were two days from port it was so bad that the escort of several four-funnel, lease-lend destroyers were forced to turn back. This was not an option for the captain and crew of the converted freighter that carried the young cadets; they ploughed on. Nine days later, on 3 February, a very relieved crew docked in New York, and the cadets rolled up their hammocks, dumped the straw mattresses that had been their beds for the previous horrific ten days and bid a hasty and heartfelt farewell to the ship.

They were now in America, but another train ride took them to their next holding station, across the border into Canada. The Canadian Air Force Establishment 31PD (Personnel Dispersal) was in Moncton, New Brunswick on the edge of the St Lawrence Seaway. There were a few changes that they could not help to notice when they got there. The barracks were centrally heated and the food was not just edible, it was good, both factors not lost on the young men recently arrived from England. Unfortunately there was a downside – boredom. After the initial lecture about the dangers of frostbite and leaving windows open at night they were left alone. There was not much to do, so they swept the floors of the two large hangars on the base, and then they swept them again, and again and again. Not surprisingly they also invaded the small town of Moncton itself whenever possible; at least it was a change of scenery, and a break from the sweeping.

As time was dragging and nothing worthwhile was happening, Bertie thought he would ask if he could re-muster into the Canadian Air Force. To no one's great surprise, especially Bertie's, his request fell on deaf ears. However, in early spring things started to happen. On 4 April a long two-day train ride south took them all to Turner Field in Georgia in the deep south of the USA, this time for a shorter wait in the hot southern sun.

On 11 April Bertie wrote to his old friend Richard Mercer back in Theodore, summarizing the journey.

> We arrived here after coming by train through Montreal and most of Ottawa to Windsor. From Windsor we went by ferry to Detroit, thence to Cincinnati, Atlanta and finally Albany. It was quite a ride, but the food on the train was OK and there were only eighteen of us and no officer. We were therefore free to do whatever we pleased . . . except miss trains.

This was to be the last holding base before flying training school. Turner Field only provided tented accommodation for the cadets, but it did boast a swimming pool and a host of sports facilities including a fully kitted gymnasium and archery range. Again the food was excellent and this time there was something to do. In the three weeks or so that they were there, Bertie and his colleagues were taught, in the American way, how to march, how to drill, and some background of the history of their new home. Strangely, however hard the instructors tried, they could not stop the British recruits from swinging their arms when they marched. Abbey Road had at least achieved that much.

On 3 May they left for Darr Aero Tech, just a few miles away near Albany, and started their flying training the very same day. It was to be an intense process; they had sixty hours of elementary flying training to fit into two months and there was no time to waste. That first day at Darr, Bertie was introduced to three new important factors in his life: Paul Soldano, who was to be his instructor for the whole of his stay at Darr Aero Tech; the PT17 Stearman, Boeing's primary trainer; and the vastness of the skies over the southern United States. Paul Soldano looked about thirty but could have been younger, and was of Italian descent. He still spoke with a very strong Italian accent despite the years in America. He also always wore a white neck scarf when flying, a legacy from an earlier accident. Paul would tell Bertie that he had broken his neck once, and did not need to have it happen a second time due to one of Bertie's silly mistakes.

It had been a full five months between stepping out of the Tiger Moth at Fairoaks and into the Stearman at Darr Aero Tech. So it came as no surprise that the first sortie was just twenty minutes, in a plane with the flight line number 18. The flight was devoted solely to lesson 4, flying straight and level. It was repeated the next day in Stearman number 28 along with lessons 16, 6, 9 and 3: climbing turns, medium turns and gliding turns, glide approach and landing, and taxiing. This added a further three-quarters of an hour to the Boulter log, and started an association with aircraft number 28 that would last the greater part of his adult life.

Even a modest ground loop the following day appeared not to disturb either him or the flying instructors charged with his tuition. He soon learned that many of his fellow pupils had performed similar unplanned manoeuvres during their first few days at Albany Field, they thought little of it and it seemed to come with the territory as far as the instructors were concerned.

The Stearman was a very basic, primary trainer by the standards of today and the instrumentation was sparse, if not virtually non-existent. Radio communication between crew and instructor was not yet considered a necessity, so a technique of passing instructions from the instructor had been devised, usually via a one-way speaking tube from instructor to pupil or by movements of the control column – one waggle meaning 'You have', the next 'I have', and two waggles meaning 'That was really wrong'.

> We thought that was a bit of a backward step for us as the Tiger Moths we had flown at Fairoaks had been fitted with two-way communication via speaking tubes: one from pilot to pupil, the other from pupil to pilot. However we soon got used to the new system and we were advised that this part of the training was to teach us to fly by the seat of our pants, by eye and by the sound of the wind in the rigging wires. To emphasize that, the rear cockpit that the students occupied had no air speed indicator.

Bertie, with Paul Soldano and number 28 flew every day for the next week, logging nearly four flying hours, revising previous exercises and adding forced landings, S-turns, steep turns, stalling and spinning to his growing repertoire of airborne accomplishments. The Stearman cockpit was starting to feel like home.

There were very few days off for the students. Darr Aero Tech was a seven-day-a-week operation. They either flew in the morning and had lectures in the afternoon or had lectures in the morning and flew in the afternoon. The pattern was simple and fixed. One day in eight was allowed for a brief respite and a short amount of non-aviation recreation in the nearby town of Albany, which boasted one cinema, several cafés and restaurants, and a roller skating rink. Above all though, it gave the cadets the opportunity to talk to people other than aviators, some of whom were actually girls! Near Albany was Radium Springs, a large parkland surrounded by trees and centred on a fabulous lagoon where they could swim, walk, sunbathe or simply talk. It was an idyllic spot to spend the brief time they had away from training.

Just once during these intensive days they were allowed a three-day pass. Armed with this they hitch-hiked to Atlanta, where the local branch of the English Speaking Union had arranged accommodation, barbecues, a swimming party and an introduction to some very heavily chaperoned local girls. They could get to the barbecue and the swimming pool but the daughters of Atlanta were definitely off-limits.

Back at Darr Aero Tech the training continued unabated. Faces changed as cadets who underperformed were sent elsewhere or 'washed-out', as the process of weeding out was referred to by both the staff and students. They left for Canada by bus on a Wednesday afternoon and were never seen or spoken of again. By 21 May, after nine hours and fifty-five minutes of dual instruction, Paul Soldano was obviously convinced that Bertie was safe enough to be let loose on his own, so prior to the second sortie of the day he got out of Stearman 28, and left LAC Boulter H.E. 1388911 to take to the skies on his first solo flight.

> Following a tradition that still holds good today, we were allowed one solo circuit each. That was all. I was both elated and apprehensive in equal measure when I was told I was ready to go solo and even more pleased with myself to bring the plane back to earth in one piece.

This set the pattern for the weeks to come. Paul would take him on a dual flight first and then they would land and Bertie would complete a solo trip, consolidating the work done on the earlier flight. By now some of the dual flights were becoming an hour in duration. So as May slipped into June during the summer of 1942, log-book totals climbed to over twenty hours' experience, and simple aerobatic manoeuvres were added to the curriculum. The second week in June added some more rather advanced aerobatics, and brought log book totals to twenty-two and a half hours dual and twelve and a half hours solo. He was already over half way to becoming a pilot.

Three flights on 18 June saw his first twenty-hour check ride by Senior Instructor P. Johnston, then it was back to more practice around the crowded skies above Albany. On the twenty-third, a one hour ten minute cross-country exercise was his first flight away from the airfield. From now on three flights a day was not uncommon and at three hours a day the time that he logged climbed rapidly towards the sixty hours' target. The twenty seventh was the date of his next check ride, this time a 35-minute sortie supervised by Lieutenant Wood. With four other flights that same day, there was just the front seat conversion ride to complete, supervised as ever by Paul Soldano. Then as suddenly as they had started, his days at Darr Aero Tech were over.

Roughly 100 miles to the north of Albany, on the route of Highway 75, lies the city of Macon. Nine miles to the south of the city on the Hawkinsville Highway, surrounded by a vast expanse of flat open farmland was Flying School Number One, Cochran Field. During the first week of July, Bertie and his fellow students with the appropriate sixty hours successfully logged were moved there for the next stage of their training. Just one week from stepping out of a Stearman in Albany, he was climbing aboard a BT13 A, more commonly known as the Vultee Valiant, with his new instructor Lt Alex Gay. As with Darr Aero Tech, Cochran Field was also a seven-day-a-week operation. The Vultee was A/C C501, which like Stearman 28 before it, was to become regularly used and to feature strongly in the initial part of Bertie's training programme at Cochran Field.

The Vultee was a modern monowing training plane, nick-named by its students 'the vibrator'. It really looked and sounded the part. It was fitted with a 450 horsepower Pratt & Whitney radial engine which meant it had twice the power that he was used to in the Stearman, and not surprisingly it was able to fly considerably faster. The Stearman's 100 miles an hour would seem sluggish compared to the Valiant's 135.

Like the PT17 before it, it had a fixed undercarriage and a wonderfully spacious cockpit, and it was considered by the top brass to be an ideal basic training plane, being generally short of vices to catch the unwary novice. It was also the first plane the students encountered that had a full radio system with the ability to talk to the ground as well as between the two-man crew; speaking tubes were history.

As was now the practice in the Arnold Scheme training system, the first lesson on 7 July was fairly short and aimed specifically at familiarizing the student with the cockpit layout and basic flying characteristics of their new training aircraft. Lesson 2, the following day, was a repeat of some of the more standard flying exercises and lasted an hour. This was to be the minimum flight time from now on unless it was a short demonstration flight with an instructor. The following week Bertie flew on ten consecutive days and logged a further ten hours and forty-five minutes. On only his seventh trip Alex Gay got out from the front seat of A/C C501 and left Bertie 'circuit-bashing' for the next hour and a half on his own. However while he was making progress, others were still being 'washed-out'. The Wednesday bus back to Canada was still being kept busy.

By 17 July the aerobatic exercises were once more being added to the training flights. This first lesson was again in A/C 501, though as the training intensified the number of aircraft identity numbers increased. Indeed, in the week from 21–29 July he never flew the same plane twice. Included in this period was a further check ride under the supervision of one of Cochran Field's senior officers, Captain (Capt.) Robert Martens. Bertie remembers Alex Gay and Robert Martens with mixed feelings.

> Alex Gay was a great chap, but he did get me as close to being 'washed-out' as I really needed to be. We got on rather well, but somehow we didn't get enough of the right work completed to the right standards at the right time. So on a check ride with Capt. Martens on 28 July it

all came to a head. I got a right royal bawling out and the Gay/Boulter team was split up and I was passed over to Lt Harold Stanhope. Again I found him a really decent sort of chap, but much more military in bearing, and described by some as 'a tough cookie'. Having said that, he was a thumping good pilot who combined these skills with a lot of fun and some excellent instructing techniques. Surprisingly he was not averse to doing things that were not in the book, particularly if they helped prove a point or explain a technique. He really instructed well on the aerobatics side of things and patiently took me through stalls, chandelles, lazy eights, slow rolls and snap rolls until they all became second nature to me; although his dive-bombing technique at night with a coke bottle was never in any official curriculum!

Again just two weeks later Bertie flew thirteen sorties in ten different aircraft in a six-day period. Life was rather busy for the British student pilots. Lt Harold Stanhope and P/O Herbert were instructors who eased his transition into the Vultee, though it would be Stanhope who would work with him through the majority of his dual training during that long, hot summer at Cochran Field. About this time, the 100 hours flown was logged, almost without comment. Just before that however on 1 August, Lt Stanhope introduced him to a totally new world – formation flying. Bertie's memories were quite vivid.

I seem to recall the instructors all wanting me to get much closer to the other planes in the small three-ship formation, whereas all my natural instincts were to keep what I thought was a reasonable distance between my plane and the others. The instructors' view of a reasonable distance and mine were often quite different. We did stream take-offs unless we all had instructors with us, then we sometimes indulged in formation take-off techniques. At this stage of our training there was always an instructor in the lead plane and the following two aircraft would attempt to fly in formation with it. The instructor would have given us all a pretty thorough briefing before take-off and we all knew what we were supposed to do, even if it proved somewhat difficult to achieve once we were airborne. Then on 15 August in A/C C532 I got to do my first solo formation. It must have gone reasonably all right as the instructors let me loose again the next day in A/C 502 on a similar solo flight. I felt pretty pleased with myself about that, I can tell you.

Night flying was started on 8 August, with a couple of exercises flown. They would soon become a more regular part of the syllabus and continue throughout the time at Cochran Field. As expected the first flight was dual, though the following two were solo. All involved just take-offs and landings. Later cross-county night exercises were added and again started with a dual flight. They initially involved following light lines positioned at 5–10 mile intervals between the airfield and the town that would be the turning point. On the second night cross-country Bertie was sent on his own. As towns were few and far between in that part of America, providing the students followed the lights and saw a town, it had to be the one they wanted; there simply weren't any others around. It was a simple system but still pretty nerve-jangling for a student pilot in the early stages of his flying career. He remembered the night solos as some of the loneliest moments of his embryo flying career. Unsurprisingly, on comparing notes with his fellow students he found that he was not the only one.

The lights of the airfield soon faded behind the plane as you headed out into the darkness, vainly looking for the string of lights you had to follow. It always seemed that the radio fell out of range even quicker than on the

daylight cross-country exercises over the same route. I
also recall that there was still a considerable amount of
ground school going on at the same time. Add to that the
regulation time in the link trainer, the PT [physical
training] and other exercise activities the US military
were keen on and you can see that there was no such
thing as spare time for any of us would-be pilots.

A further check ride on 14 August, under the supervision
of Capt. Sather, saw him and some of his colleagues cleared
for dual student flights known as team rides. This
entailed two cadets taking the plane and carrying out the
required exercise, one as pilot and one as observer. They then
changed seats and roles, and repeated the same exercise.
These team rides would soon become a regular feature of
their training programme. Alan Edwards was the first
colleague to share such an exercise with him. There would be
eleven such team-ride flights in the next nine days, as cadets
William Bishop, John Bellis, Cyril Barton and Peter Booth-
Smith joined Bertie. He and Peter were to fly together many
more times before the course ended and they struck up a firm
friendship in the process.

In addition to this, the first real cross-country flights were
undertaken in the new plane and over new territory. Having
spent weeks flying frequent sorties of between forty-five and
seventy-five minutes, the arrival of cross-country trips of two
hours fifteen minutes and two hours twenty-five minutes was
definitely breaking new ground. The first one for Bertie
was with Harold Stanhope from Cochran to Milled Gaville to
Cochran 2, then on to Butler and Griffin and back to Cochran.
Two days later it was from Cochran to Greenwood and back
to Cochran. Then suddenly the dual cross-country instruction
was completed and the following day, 23 August, it was time
for the solo cross-country from Cochran to Cochran 2 and
back. There was no let up; the next day saw the first night
cross-country and a further two hours fifteen minutes were
added to both the night-flying and grand total of hours flown.

The turning point for this exercise was the town of Waycross, an interesting place on the edge of the notorious Okefenokee Swamp, one of the largest areas of swamp and wetland in the United States. At the time, to Bertie and his fellow cadets, it was just a vast dark area without lights a few miles south of the town, and definitely a no-go area for a single-engined aircraft flown by a student pilot.

Four days and nine flights later Capt. Robert Martens had seen enough and signed Bertie's log-book indicating that a further change of airfield and plane was due. So Bertie headed off south for his first introduction to Napier Field, Alabama, and the legendry advanced trainer, the North American AT6 Harvard (or Texan as it was referred to by the US contingent at the airfield). Napier Field was located close to the city of Dothan, in the deep south of Alabama, just 25 miles from the state border on the Florida panhandle and 50 or so flying miles from the Gulf of Mexico. Again it was perfect flying territory and they were blessed with almost perfect flying weather. The only major problem was the tendency of fierce thunderstorms to develop rapidly in the area; blundering into one of those whilst night flying would certainly have disastrous consequences. Indeed several cadet pilots were lost in this manner during the years of training at Napier Field.

Once installed in the Harvard it was the increase in cruise speed that Bertie noticed first. With the PT17 everything happened at 90 to 100 miles an hour, with the Vultee it had been about 130. Now, following his first conversion to type exercise, carefully noted in the log-book as forty minutes of transition on 9 September with Lt Tyrrell, he was confronted with the Harvard's ability to cruise comfortably at 160–170 miles an hour. Even at that speed there were still a further 30 or more available if it was needed. However docile, it was still quite a beast for a student pilot to handle, having nearly three times the power output of the Stearman. Needless to say all the other flying characteristics, in common with each of the previous training planes, had improved and increased in line with its speed. The progression to the Harvard seemed natural.

Once the first week at Napier Field was completed, the single flight per day soon gave way to two, then three or sometimes four. On the 28 September, he logged nearly four hours in four different planes practising both his instrument flying and his formation flying. Even with all this time airborne, the ground school continued unabated. Then with a portent of things to come, the frequency of long night-navigation cross-country and night-formation exercises intensified. Between 2 and 9 October between nine and ten hours was devoted entirely to night flights covering these lessons. On the 30th he was again paired up with Peter Booth-Smith on a team ride covering more instrument work. As well as the many trips together on the Vultee, they had flown together a couple of weeks earlier in the Harvard when Peter had acted as safety pilot while Bertie had his head buried in the cockpit, practising flying on instruments.

It was during the team rides that the 200 hours figure was reached in his log-book, and incredible as it may have seemed to him at the time, his stay at Napier Field was also rapidly coming to a conclusion, though not before a team ride with Peter Booth–Smith had written off one of the beautiful Harvards in a spectacular crash on the Napier Field runway. It also reminded them of the harsh discipline imposed under the West Point style of training.

It had been a good day and we had completed the task set. I was scrabbling about behind my seat looking for the log to complete the paperwork and thus be ready for another rapid departure. We were settled down on our final approach and had just flared to land when the guy in the tower screamed through the radio at us, 'Ship 419 give it the gun – give it the gun!' With no hesitation whatsoever Peter gave it the gun as instructed. With full flap and trimmed precisely for approach speed and landing, 419 reared up vertically like an over-excited stallion. My mind was instantly distracted from the flying log as my entire field of vision filled with the blue of the Florida sky; we flicked left at what seemed a near vertical angle and runway replaced sky. The noise was tremendous as we arrived at full chat. I can still remember to this day the vision of both wheels, complete with oleos ascending in a graceful arc either side of the canopy at the moment of impact with the runway. It then fell totally silent. Luckily we both emerged without a scratch though Peter's pride was badly dented by the experience. We were just standing about looking at the wreckage as the crash crews arrived. For his sins, Peter was ordered to carry around with him a Harvard wheel on a chain round his neck for the next two weeks. We thought this very harsh, yet to the instructors it was normal.

Three days later, on 16 October he was at Eglin Field, Florida, on a gunnery course. In five days flat and with the very modest expenditure of just 1,100 rounds of ammunition, spread over eleven hours, Lts Weaver and Wyman and P/Os Bell and Barr taught him all they thought he needed to know about aerial gunnery. On the 20th he was sent back to Napier Field for the last eight days of his pilot training. When he clambered out of Harvard N432 on 3 November, he did not know that he would not fly again for nearly four months, and that when he did it would be back in England in the DH 2A Tiger Moth. That last single one-hour simulated combat mission in early November brought this phase of his training to a close. It also earned him an impressive array of official stamps, signatures and countersignatures from Major Simpson, Capt. Larrabee and F.A. Parsons, OC Training Group One.

Just over a week later on 10 November, there was a graduation ceremony in the post chapel at Napier Field. Following an address and presentation of a diploma confirming his completion of the Course in Army Air Forces Advanced

Flying by Col James L Daniel Jr., the CO of the Air Corps, Major Charles G. Simpson Jr. presented Bertie with his wings. It was now official. He had made it. He was a pilot. His stay in America was over. It was time to get back to England, there was a war to fight.

CHAPTER THREE

Back to England

As we have seen, it was almost a further four months before Bertie was to find himself back in the cockpit of an aircraft again. From Napier Field there was the long, tiring and somewhat torturous journey home. He retraced his steps by train back to Moncton, New Brunswick, where there was a ten-day wait until space aboard the luxury liner *Queen Elizabeth* (now converted to a troop carrier) was available for the voyage back to England. Time here was spent relaxing, ice skating and enjoying ham, eggs and chips in the café close to the Moncton Ice Rink. If the days in training had gone quickly, then the ten days' relaxation in Canada were even quicker. Although the *Queen Elizabeth* was as crowded as the converted freighter on the outward journey, it was a very different, more comfortable vessel to travel in because of its heritage as a transatlantic liner. The gods of the weather also smiled on their journey home, which was considerably smoother than the outward crossing, and was accomplished this time in just six days.

The *Queen Elizabeth* docked in Southampton in the early morning and amazingly they were billeted in the Grand Hotel in Harrogate by the time night fell, having been transported halfway across the country by the hard-pressed rail system. The Grand itself was full of newly qualified pilots, all back from the USA and Canada, and all eagerly awaiting a posting for further training.

We were packed six to a room, and for most of the new pilots the conversations were all based around the 'Where do you think you will go?' subject. Needless to say we all wanted to be fighter pilots, and certainly we all thought we were up to it, mainly based upon the fact that we had all actually managed to survive the course and we had all proved to our instructors that we could fly the Harvard. I remember that we speculated that in reality there had probably been a 40 per cent 'wash-out' rate amongst cadets. Looking back I don't think we were far wrong. Some of those who were dropped from the course in America were able to continue their pilot training in Canada, others retrained as navigators, flight engineers or wireless operators. Whilst at Harrogate we attended lectures and did a lot of PT. We also got leave. Like most of the other lads I took leave and grabbed the opportunity to go home for a few days and to see my mother. It was hard to believe that I had been away from Norwich for nearly a year.

A week or so later we were sent to Whitley Bay, on the cold, wet and windy Northumberland coast. There we were to remain billeted in a row of large, cold, seafront houses about ten to a house, while we were taught to play at being soldiers on the local golf course, where a mini-commando course had been set up. We drilled, we marched, we exercised, we shot guns and we got to throw live grenades! Then for light relief and to get away from the golf course, we went on long distance route marches . . . all meant to toughen us up, or at least that's what we were told.

We also went on leave again. Unofficially we learned to scavenge for whatever we needed, and we became very good at it. The houses were so cold that we were not averse to commandeering our neighbours' gates and fences to use to fuel the open fires on those long, cold winter evenings. Anything burnable was deemed fair game! Our disregard for the law was directly linked to the drop in temperature and the depth of the snow.

By 25 February the misery of Whitley Bay had come to an end and several of the pilots, including Bertie, were posted to No. 7 EFTS (Elementary Flying Training School) at RAF Desford. Desford was located only a few fields away from the site of the present-day Mallory Park motor-racing circuit in Leicestershire and was home to a refamiliarization course on the DH 82A Tiger Moth. The 28th saw three flights for Bertie in Tiger Moth N651. Two dual sorties with Sgt Collinson were flown and a brief ten-minute re-solo was authorized as his last flight of the day. Sgt Collinson was another instructor whose style and approach to instructing appealed to him.

He was somewhat older, probably about twenty-seven or twenty-eight, and was a bit of an older brother figure to the young, inexperienced pilots in his charge. He de-Americanized us and taught us to fly the English way. He smoothed us out and he removed the sharp edges that were so beloved by the American instructors; and he concentrated on aerobatic manoeuvres. It was soon obvious that this was an area somewhat neglected by the US training system, almost certainly sacrificed in order to turn out as many pilots as it did in such a short time. Sgt Collinson had a refresher programme that corrected that. However my first aerobatic lesson was a disaster. The first slow roll to the right went fairly well but five seconds later the requested slow roll to the left became a total nightmare as the allowance for the torque reaction of the engine was not put in place and the whole manoeuvre went horribly wrong. The situation was recovered by Sgt Collinson, who then went on to explain what had gone wrong with such a simple, basic manoeuvre and how to prevent it from happening again. The Harvard was not as twitchy as the Tiger Moth and I had forgotten that. I still had a lot to learn.

I recall feeling that the Tiger Moths at Desford were a bit of a come-down compared to the Harvards. Their performance was vastly inferior and their cockpit instrumentation was decidedly primitive. N651 had a turn-and-slip indicator with a needle instead of the more modern turn-and-bank instrument with a ball, it had no artificial horizon, no DI [directional indicator] and just a horizontally mounted magnetic compass. Some of the Moths were not even fitted with an ASI [air speed indicator]. Instead they were equipped with the earlier indicator system that simply had a hinged flap of aluminium on one wing with a scale behind it. The faster you flew, the further back the flap got pushed by the airflow and the pilot (or instructor) could then read the speed from the scale.

That was the downside. The upside for me was that Desford itself was a small, friendly operation and only ever seemed to have fifty or so pilots there at any one time, so the instruction became personal and more thorough. Having said that, accidents did happen and a check ride that I had with F/Lt Vaughan midway through the course ended up with the poor old Tiger Moth with its nose through a hedge. We were more or less OK but the poor old Moth was out of service for a while. The PFL [practice forced landing] went awry when the engine failed to respond to the instructor's command for power when we were down to 150 feet and that fast-looming Leicestershire hedge began rapidly to fill our field of vision, concentrate our minds and eventually bring the aircraft to a rather undignified halt. It was altogether a timely head-shrinking exercise for a Harvard 'ace'.

The first day of March was a busy one; three more flights, again two dual and one solo, added a further three hours to the now almost full log-book. The 3rd was the same, except the total time in the air was three hours and thirty-five minutes. On the fourth day at Desford came the hedge incident. F/Lt Vaughan was the examiner for Bertie's passenger flying test, this time in A/C DE 298. Having survived the hedge, a further passenger flying test followed the next day in DE589, then it was back to N6651, more practice and the start of cross-country navigation exercises in England. The first of these (Ex V11 in the log-book) was on 6 March and was the last of four sorties flown that day. With Sgt Bottom along for the ride, Bertie took off from Desford and headed west for some 30 miles (about fifteen to twenty minutes' flight time), past the sprawling town of Tamworth spread out on either side of the main A5 trunk road and, over the Grand Union Canal, to turn overhead Lichfield and head back east. The route then passed to the north of Leicester, over the town of Melton Mowbray and back to the airfield at Desford once more to complete the exercise. The whole flight covered some 94 miles and took just one hour and ten minutes.

Three days later he repeated the exercise with Sgt Boles, and on 10 March he took P/O Woodall on a slightly longer trip around the Midlands countryside, visiting Derby and Oakham before returning to base. That was a further one hour and thirty minutes to add to the hours flown; which were now climbing towards the 250 mark. Every day saw either three or four flights, until on 12 March a memorable six separate exercises were flown, totalling a full five hours in the air. His log-book shows that, unsurprisingly, he then had two days off. Three more revision exercises soon after this brought his grand total up to 247 hours and fifty minutes, which completed all the available space in his first log-book. He then went to the flight office to collect his second; another milestone had been reached. A mixture of day and night flying filled the remainder of the month until the 24th, when his posting came through. He was off to No. 20 (P) Advance Flying Unit (AFU) at RAF Kidlington, just a few miles to the north of the university city of Oxford.

It was there that on 7 April, he had got the opportunity to fly a twin-engined aircraft for the first time. V3859 was an

Airspeed Oxford, equipped with two 350 horsepower radial engines. Although this was more power than he had ever had under his throttle hand before, the extra weight and bulk of the Oxford did not allow for a particularly sparkling performance. Despite being a little livelier than the Tiger Moth in the speed department, its performance was somewhat below that of the Harvard, and more or less comparable with the Vultee. However being a cabin-class aircraft, it did not have the same manoeuvrability as any of the types he had previously encountered.

Flight Sergeant (F/Sgt) Whitehead spent a couple of hours on 7 and 8 April introducing Bertie to flying twins in general and the Oxford in particular. Three flights later, on the 10th, he went solo for the first time in a multi-engined aircraft. He was also reintroduced to the joys of the Link trainer at RAF Croughton, located a few miles on the opposite side of Oxford.

The Airspeed Oxford was a much larger aircraft than anything we had flown before. Obviously it was the first multi-engined plane that any of us had flown, but it really was an easy aircraft to fly. It was a twin with fixed-pitch propellers and a fixed undercarriage. Whether by design or accident, the docile nature of the Oxford was ably demonstrated to me on one of my first conversion flights when my instructor insisted on putting one hand in his pocket on take-off and leaving it there until we reached cruise altitude, flying the whole of the way single handed. I can recall thinking either this was a very cavalier attitude or he had supreme confidence in his aircraft. Looking back I suspect it was a mixture of both. It did however serve to demonstrate to me the fact that this was an easy and forgiving plane to fly. In fact it seemed to almost land itself it was so docile. Added to this I never once experienced or heard of an engine failure on an Oxford at any of the units I flew with. It really was a very good plane to use to introduce new pilots to multi-engined flying and to hour-build and enhance their confidence.

Fifty-two flights later he was deemed satisfactory to send to Norfolk, to 1519 Beam Approach Training Flight, RAF Feltwell. The log-book entries do not show any room for leave between these postings, just one day for travelling from Kidlington to Feltwell. There was not even a chance to pop home, even though Norwich was only 25–30 miles away.

Standard beam approach worked like this. The runways fitted with the system had a transmitter that gave out three distinct radio signals that the beam approach unit on the plane converted to radio signals. The signal for being correctly aligned on the runway was a steady single note. If you were the one side of the runway it gave out the letter A in Morse code, 'dit-dah'; if you were on the other it signalled N, 'dah-dit'. It was a narrow beam that widened out the further away from the runway you were. Added to the standard approach beam was an outer and inner marker system that were also audio signals. The outer marker which we aimed to reach at 600 feet on the corrected altimeter barometric setting, gave out a 'caw-caw-caw' signal and the inner marker, which we had to reach at 150 feet was a very rapid 'dit-dit-dit' signal. As this was a blind approach aid and not a landing system, it had to be hoped that at 150 feet the runway would be visible. Training was what you expected, practice, practice and more practice. We all knew that one day we would need to use it for real. It was therefore a challenge to get really good at it, and as a bonus it provided us with some really serious instrument flying practice.

Three weeks later it was all over. Like everything else in the RAF pilot training schedule, it seemed to go past very rapidly. So after two weeks' leave, on 8 June Sgt H.E. Boulter was posted to his first unit as a staff pilot. He went to No. 11 Radio School, Hooton Park, situated on the northern edge of the Wirral peninsula, a few miles inland from the Irish Sea, just south of Liverpool.

I was really looking forward to this, as Hooton Park was equipped with both the Avro Anson and the Blackburn Botha. The Anson was a relatively new aircraft, having been in service for just over six years. The Botha however was even newer, having only become operational in late 1939, some four years earlier. To us it was a totally new aircraft, and we were sure we would get to fly them both. The Anson was fairly similar in size and performance to the Oxford and if anything even more docile; in fact it was a real airborne gentleman's carriage. Like the Oxford it had a fixed pitch propeller, but had progressed to a retractable undercarriage. The main obvious difference to the pupil was the fact that there were no dual control variants available. When you flew it for the first time you sat in the pilot's seat and the instructor sat in his seat and yelled instructions and advice at you across a rather roomy cockpit. You did all the flying, and that included raising and lowering the undercarriage with its 180 turns on the crank handle.

The 8th of June was very busy – in fact for Bertie it really started on the evening of the 7th. He had taken his bicycle with him, which proved a particularly wise move. Hooton Park was furnished with a pair of tarmac runways, the longest being 2,500 yards long with its starter extension. It ran parallel and rather close to the River Mersey, with the Manchester Ship Canal squeezed in between. Needless to say when using the cross runway in a northerly direction the crew's field of vision was entirely filled with the river and canal. The huge Bowater's factory sat at the eastern end of the main runway along with its 200 foot high chimney, which acted as an ideal identifier for incoming aircraft in bad or even marginal visibility. Contemporary paperwork listed it as an aviation hazard; the pilots operating from Hooton Park often found it rather a bonus.

Upon reporting to the sergeants' mess, he was sent to his temporary billet on the outskirts of the airfield. It was in a requisitioned private house, converted to two-man rooms for the new aircrew at the station, and quite a distance from the main airfield buildings. The bike was used to transport him back to the mess for dinner and an evening in the bar. If dinner was good, the bar after dinner was even better. Bertie was introduced to the questionable delights of Irish whiskey, the flavour of which gained instant approval. A couple of hours and several drinks later he and the trusty bicycle headed back to bed. Away from the mess he rode, down the road, along the lane, up the garden path and into the garage. Thinking that he was still more or less in control of matters he then dismounted, only to find that his arms and legs were no longer under his command and that in fact the bike itself has been mainly responsible for their safe return to the billet. A couple of his new colleagues found him a little later in the flower garden, which was as far as he had been able to crawl unaided. He was assisted to bed, loudly telling anyone who would listen that he had an Anson to fly the next day and was not in a fit state to crawl into the cockpit of the plane, never mind fly it. Of course no one listened; they had heard it all before, and from the mouths of weaker souls than him. He was donated a recently emptied fire bucket by his new friends for emergency use, and told he would feel all right in the morning. Much to his astonishment he did.

Two type-familiarization flights were undertaken in Anson N9717 that morning followed by three solo flights, amounting to two hours and fifty minutes. He was then immediately moved to Anson DJ168 and with a three-man crew on board he started his job as a staff pilot, flying radio operators as they learned and perfected their skills as anti-surface-vessel radar operators. The object of the exercise was to find a freighter or similar vessel for the trainees to home in on, though this could cause a little consternation as some were armed and more than a little trigger happy and did not much like being tracked by an aircraft dodging in and out of cloud. Pilots had to be aware that a steep 180 degree turn might be required, in addition to firing the colours of the day to keep out of trouble. Crews consisted of the pilot, a wireless operator and radar instructor and two wireless operator pupils. By that same evening, when he returned to the mess for supper, he calculated that he had flown seven hours and twenty-five minutes in that first day. It was a real blessing that he had not had the hangover he so richly deserved.

This flying programme was to be the pattern of his life for the next few months, except that after a few weeks into the posting, accommodation was found for him and Sgt Bell in the sergeants' mess, and there was no longer any need for that cycle ride several times a day. Sgt Bell was an avid beer drinker, so the pattern of mess life continued in the familiar RAF style. Also by then, work was starting to settle down into a regular routine. A typical route for the training flights would be to coast out over the Irish Sea at the mouth of the River Dee and then take a northerly turn to run parallel to the Lancashire coast up to Barrow-in-Furness. From there it was a westerly heading towards the Isle of Man then south down the centre of the Irish Sea towards Anglesey to pick up an easterly track to the mainland and to land back at Hooton Park, making sure to identify the River Dee, not the Mersey only a few miles to the north. It was a simple mistake, often made by most of the new pilots, including Bertie, on their first solo flights in the Anson.

Once the crew got a positive fix on the tall factory chimney at the end of the runway the plane was all but home. On a good day they also got a clear view of Mt Snowdon, though flying into Snowdonia was strongly discouraged, for obvious reasons. On 28 and 29 August Sgt Hay and his crew in Botha L6454 got it wrong and paid the ultimate price. Bertie and F/Sgt Roe, along with several other crews, spent the next two days searching the area in Bothas looking for the crash site.

He logged five hours on his share of the search and rescue mission. On the second day, one of the other search planes, sent up while his plane was being refuelled, eventually located the wreck on the upper slopes of the remote Llwytmor Mountain. It was then left to the Llandwrog Mountain Rescue Service to complete the recovery mission, and the airborne teams returned to base.

So busy was Hooton Park at the time, that, having completed three hours and twenty-five minutes on the search and rescue effort on its second day, he was airborne again within the hour in an Anson, performing his usual flying duties as a staff pilot. On an exceptionally clear day Belfast was visible if the route chosen took him close to Anglesey. There were also days when the visibility was right down to instrument conditions; nevertheless the training had to go on, there was no let up. Neither human tragedy nor weather could stop it.

> The training flights were always better than the solo ones. Firstly you had company, but more importantly you had someone to crank that infernal undercarriage. It was operated by a crank handle to the right of the pilot's seat. One hundred and eighty turns up and one hundred and eighty turns down. Two green knobs indicated the undercarriage was down and locked and a red light indicated it was not locked down. Trainee radar operators were really good at cranking handles as I recall, and it was amazing how important it was, we told them, for the pilot to really concentrate on his flying at that stage of the flight, and not be distracted by the need to wind the handle. Fortunately I think all the pilots told the same story, so it got to being believed by most of the radar trainees passing through the school.

On 29 July, a month before the search and rescue mission, there was a brief change to routine when he was introduced for the first time to the unloved Blackburn Botha. An altogether larger aircraft than the Anson, it was considered underpowered, despite having two Bristol Perseus radial engines pushing out 930 horsepower each, compared to the 335 available from each of the Cheetahs on the Anson. The fact that it was twice as heavy may well have been fundamental to its problems. He flew one sortie on 29 July with Sgt Theophilus, conducting an air test in L6241, little knowing that six weeks later under the guidance of F/Lt March he would convert to it and remain on that type throughout the winter until he was posted to No. 12 (P) AFU, Grantham, in July 1944.

He liked the Botha, as it seemed a more complex aircraft and more the sort of thing he wanted to get his hands on. At a mess party a short while later he mentioned in conversation to S/Ldr Hole, the OC No. 11 Radio School, that he was rather bored with the Anson and would like to fly the Botha as it seemed a more advanced aircraft and would be a new challenge. S/Ldr Hole was not one to let an opportunity pass and just a few days later Bertie was transferred.

> The Botha was a front-line torpedo bomber relegated to second-line training duties. It had been in this role just over a year when I got to fly it on a regular basis. I particularly remember getting in through the side door and walking forward along the low, narrow corridor between the starboard hull and the torpedo-bay wall. It was on that wall incidentally that the fuel management panel was located, fortunately it was always set prior to flight. Even at 5 foot 5 I had to stoop to pass along this corridor; the taller chaps must have been bent double. Like the Anson before it there was no dual-control training version available to us at Hooton Park, so it was the same scenario as before; I sat in the left-hand seat and the instructor sat in his and shouted at me. I was getting used to being shouted at on my conversion flights.
>
> The starting sequence on the Perseus engines was

operated by the Coffman cartridge system. I distinctly recall being shown this on my first trip. I was also shown the wire to pull that rotated the cartridge holder to activate the next cartridge, should the engine not fire up on the first attempt. I was told then that it did not work on the plane we were in. What I was not told that it did not work on any of the planes at Hooton Park. Whether it did on any of the other Bothas that were ever built, I never knew. On all of ours, positioning the holder was a manual operation carried out by the ground crew, or the pilot if no member of the ground crew was available. I remember doing it once on an airfield not familiar with Bothas. It was quite a fag getting out of my seat, scuttling down the corridor, out to the reluctant engine, clambering onto the wheel to rotate the cartridge holder, then retracing my steps back into the cockpit for a second go. After it had caught me out once I always made sure I gave the primer one extra pump before attempting to start the engine. That always did it.

The start up itself was always quite a smoky affair. There was the initial puff of smoke from the Coffman cartridge itself that drifted out of the engine cowling, then a much larger, denser, cloud from the exhaust of the engine as it kicked into life. From the cockpit, it always seemed as if the engines were shrouded in smoke for the first twenty or thirty seconds once they were started. I also recall being told that the poor old Botha simply could not fly on one engine, it merely flattened out the glide angle and gave you a greater choice of fields to put the plane into. Fortunately my Bristol Perseus engines never let me down once and I never had to find out for myself. The Botha had constant-speed propellers and a retractable undercarriage, so that we felt we were flying real aeroplanes with all the trick bits. Added to that we were quite an oddity in the wartime RAF, as we were a daytime, 9–5.30 sort of operation as there was no night flying at Hooton, certainly none that

I ever took part in, and homing onto shipping at night would have been suicidal. It was quite a comfortable life, all things considered.

It was on one of the many routine trips out over the Irish Sea that I saw my first Mosquito. We came across a Miles Master towing a target drogue. This Mosquito came in from the rear quarter of the drogue to fire at it. Compared to the Mosquito the Master was slow. The Mosquito pilot misjudged the difference in speed and approached too fast, necessitating a severe late turn to the left that must have caused him to black out. The plane continued to roll left and spiralled down into the sea. We quickly radioed back to Hooton and dropped down to 50 feet but all we saw was one wheel and a small oil slick and matchwood floating on the surface.

Bertie's last flight on the Botha was on 17 May, in L6187, an aircraft that he had flown several times before. It followed the routine that he had flown for the previous year and was as uneventful as were most of his flights from Hooton Park. He was promoted to pilot officer and given an above-average rating, his time at Hooton Park was at an end.

He was granted a few weeks' leave prior to taking up residence at Grantham. He had completed a full year at No. 11 Radio School and added close to 600 hours to his log-book whilst there. But Grantham had better things to offer, not least of which was the Bristol Blenheim.

CHAPTER FOUR

Blenheims
and Mosquitos

Situated less than 2 miles east of Grantham, RAF Spittlegate was a grass airfield left over from World War I. It was altogether a much larger operation than Hooton Park, having four times the number of personnel stationed there at any one time. It also had the bonus of a large contingent of Women's Auxiliary Air Force personnel (WAAFs) – there were almost as many WAAFs at Spittlegate as there were total staff at Hooton, a fact not lost on the young pilots.

It had reinforced matting designating the east–west runway, with just one cross runway heading more or less north-east to south-west. As with his previous posting at Hooton Park, there was no permanent electrical runway lighting available, but there was a gooseneck flare system in place on the main runway, which was in constant use.

> I remember getting lost on a night cross-country exercise while I was training on the Blenheim. I can hardly blame the standard of runway lighting on my dilemma that morning, but a battery of electrical lights might well have helped. I was just returning to the airfield as dawn was starting to break. There was a ground mist and although I thought I was almost in the overhead, the tower kept insisting that I continued to fly the same QDM (Magnetic Bearing to a Direction Finding Station)

heading. It was only when I told the tower his radio transmissions were becoming fainter that he realized I had overshot. At exactly the same time I saw a red flare burst through the morning mist in front of me. I dived through the mist to be greeted by the sight of a large airfield with what looked like dozens of B17 Flying Fortress bombers all assembling in preparation for take-off. I did a quick low-level approach and dived for the runway. At a couple of hundred feet I remembered that one of our instructors had reminded us that the Blenheim looked awfully similar to the Junkers Ju88. I prayed that the airfield's defences were either on the ball with their silhouette recognition or too busy watching their own planes preparing for take-off. Either way I made it, got marshalled in, treated royally with a superb American-style breakfast and refuelled before the mist cleared sufficiently to make the twenty-minute return flight to Spittlegate. It was my one and only visit to the USAAF at Grafton Underwood.

The Blenheim was in theory quite a different animal than the Botha. Despite its reputation I got on pretty much OK with the Botha, but it really wasn't a patch on the Blenheim. The Blenheim was altogether a sleeker-looking machine and with a weight saving of over 4,000 pounds and similar power available from its Bristol Mercury engines, it had almost 20 miles an hour speed advantage. As it happened the Botha also lost out when you compared its range and operational ceiling capabilities, not that it mattered. The only area where the Blenheim came second was in the bomb-load capability, and that was rather academic as the Botha only ever went operational with 608 Squadron that I recall, and that only lasted about a year. It then got relegated to second line duties, which is of course where I encountered it.

Having said all that, I did not find it a great deal different to the Botha. Nicer perhaps, but if I had come to it straight from the Oxford, as many of the chaps did, then I have no doubt it would have been quite a big and noticeable jump forward, though it did have its idiosyncrasies to catch the unwary newboy. It did not like a rapid throttle opening on take-off, and much preferred the pilot to take his time to get to full throttle fully open. If not, it was not averse to producing a rich-cut situation, killing both the engines. The ensuing drama of aborting the run or gliding it down to the end of the runway and seeing if the brakes and tyres were capable of stopping it from careering off the end was, I'm told, an extremely focusing experience for all concerned. If, however, it was a single engine that failed, then perhaps the situation was in many ways worse. The swing that it produced was quite violent, and positive and accurate corrective action was immediately needed to prevent a total disaster. These actions usually included putting the nose down to increase speed and decreasing the power from the good engine to prevent the plane rolling over on its back through the asymmetric forces working on it. It also usually required the retraction of the undercarriage to cut down the drag. With one engine out and an immediate return to earth imminent, these were not necessarily the instinctive actions for most pilots, especially an unwary newcomer faced with the problem for the first time. Regretfully for some it would also be the last. The correct choice of response under these circumstances was vital for survival.

Should it have been the port engine that failed, then an immediate loss of hydraulic pressure could be expected to add to the pilot's headaches. However all was not inevitably lost as the rudder was large and very effective to counter the swing from asymmetric flight. The rudder trim was servo-assisted and was quickly able to relieve the pressure from the pilot's leg that was countering the swing. As such, 'touch and go' circuit training was not permitted.

The cockpit layout was not that well planned in my

view. On occasions you needed to have three or even four hands to keep her in check and do your job. On other occasions, you needed hands that were also armour-plated to protect them from getting knocked about and skinned from bits and pieces in the cockpit. The awkwardness of the fuel-tank selector was a real case in point and a total pig to reach and operate; as were several other controls, especially the handles that operated the engines cooling gills. These were identical to look at and feel, and yet were placed together at the right rear of the pilot's seat. They were both awkward to get at and operate and yet it was essential in the event of engine failure on take-off to open the correct one to prevent your one good engine from cooking-up and overheating. As the old joke said, apart from that sort of thing it was quite a nice plane.

On 11 July P/O Osborne spent fifty minutes introducing Bertie to the Blenheim Mk V. The following day a further type-familiarization sortie took place for nearly one and a half hours, before P/O Osborne jumped out to let F/Lt Bonakis conduct his solo check on type. This was not the end of Bertie's day's work, and two further solos of forty and fifty-five minutes followed the same afternoon. Somewhat to his surprise P/O Osborne then clambered back on board to spend almost another hour introducing him to further elements of the Blenheim's characteristics. A note in his log-book signed that same day confirmed that F/Sgt Gordon Blackie had also instructed him on the various drills on starting and stopping the huge Mercury radial engines. Bertie's signature under a similar note confirmed that he had understood. It was quite a significant day's work; five trips and nearly five hours in the air, as well as the ground instruction. The magic 1,000 hours log-book entry was fast approaching.

Three weeks later as the August sun made life quite bearable in rural Lincolnshire the emphasis of the training shifted to night flying – not bad when you think about it, for an airfield without any permanent runway lighting. By 24 August there was a return to daylight flying and six days of more beam approach training (BAT) and the link at 1536 BAT Flight, who fortunately shared the airfield at Spittlegate with Bertie's unit. He logged five hours in those six days. This BAT posting also brought about a brief but rather pleasant re-acquaintance with the Airspeed Oxford. Once that was over, it was back to the Blenheim.

The last trip in the Blenheim was a night sortie on 11 September and earned him yet another stamp in his log-book, signed by no less a mortal than the wing commander in charge of No. 12 ATU himself, proclaiming that his proficiency was above average as a pilot on type. It did strike Bertie as more than a little ironic that it was noted that he had above average proficiency on an aircraft type that he was unlikely ever to fly again, but he put that to the back of his mind, as combat flying was coming ever closer.

RAF Warboys was still a fairly new airfield when he arrived on 9 September. It had been completed less than three years earlier, and compared with some of his previous postings it still seemed very new, as of course were the rows of de Havilland Mosquito Mk IVs scattered around the airfield.

I remember looking at them and thinking to myself, 'Well I've got here at last. My God, that's a real aeroplane', and it really was. I had read up the notes provided by the RAF to all squadron pilots. With a top speed approaching 400 miles an hour, a service ceiling of nearly 35,000 feet and a range of nearly 1,800 miles, this was an altogether different animal from anything I had ever flown. It really was a going to be a case of higher, further and faster, and all very exciting.

He would, however, have to curb his enthusiasm and wait almost three weeks before he got his hands on one of the T3 training aircraft. In the meantime he did manage to complete five bombing practice sorties in assorted Oxfords of 1655 MTU. These flights raised his log-book entries to 997 hours and twenty-five minutes. He would therefore achieve his 1,000 hours on a Mosquito, and by pure chance it was to be on his first solo flight aboard HJ853 on 28 September, his second day with the unit and the plane. The T3 Mosquito was a dual-control machine and therefore conversion was a slightly more orthodox affair than with Bothas and Blenheims. The first two type-conversion flights on the T3 were with S/Ldr Buckley DFC, a man not much older than Bertie himself, but well experienced in flying the Mosquito and already with a deco-rated combat career behind him. He knew the plane well.

The total daylight dual training for Bertie was just short of four and a half hours.

The plane itself was a total joy to fly. The whole thing seemed much lighter on the controls and more respon-sive than anything I had flown before; everything seemed superbly co-ordinated and balanced. The nearest plane I could compare it to was the Harvard back in pilot training in America, nothing else came close. I had no difficulty making the plane do any of the manoeuvres that my instructor asked. I could not believe how good it really was. The increased power, speed and manoeuvrability all seemed pretty easy to cope with. The real problem was slowing the darned thing down enough to commence the landing and recovery procedures into the airfield. It was such a slip-pery plane compared to anything we had experienced before. We could be operating at well over 300 miles an hour, then have to lose over 200 to join the circuit and get down to landing speed at 130 miles per hour. It didn't help matters that the flap-limiting speed was 150. I remember imagining to myself that it must have been very similar to flying the Spitfire, not of course that I had ever been fortunate enough to have the oppor-tunity to make the comparison.

For the remainder of the week I practised in the T3 all the basic flying procedures that were needed to become combat ready. I did quite a lot of single-engine work, sometimes with the 'dead' engine feathered, sometimes with it unfeathered. Then there were single-engine landings and single-engine flapless landings. I remember thinking that if anything worse happened than having one engine not working and having the flaps shot out, then the arrival was going to be decidedly interesting. Talk in the crew room and mess confirmed my own initial thoughts. There would be no recovery procedures from an engine failure with a full bomb load and a full load of fuel immediately after take-off. At full power in this situation the aircraft would roll on to its back regardless of full rudder and aileron input. It was considered that the best thing to do was almost certainly to cut the good engine and attempt to land straight ahead in what had become a heavyweight glider. I'm not aware of anyone ever pulling it off. We did hear of crashes on take-off, though there were seldom any survivors to ask the appropriate questions. That somehow confirmed our views.

I completed the month with some instrument flying on the 29th and some night work on the 30th and a strong feeling that I still had quite a lot to learn.

Although he did not know it at the time, the thirty-five minute night dual-conversion flight with S/Ldr Buckley was to be his last dual flight before going operational. All the remainder of the learning required for the post of bomber pilot would be 'on the job training'. The next week 1655 MTU moved 2½ miles down the A141 to RAF Wyton, a similar airfield in many ways to Warboys. It had between 2,000 and 2,500 personnel, three decent concrete runways, and was fully equipped for operational night flying. That said, it was different in the fact that it was a pre-war aerodrome and luxurious compared to Warboys and its Nissen huts. Once at

Wyton the training planes that were allocated to 1655 MTU were the Mk IV and The Mk XX.

I remember the day all the new pilots and all the new navigators were called into one of the squadron meeting rooms. We were told to mix and chat and basically pair up with someone and 'make up your own crew'. The idea was to find someone who you felt you could work with, have a chat and see if he felt the same, and that really was about it. It was all a bit of a novel experience for us chaps, who had spent the past few years being trained instinctively to follow orders and do as you were told. However unusual the selection system may have appeared, it seemed to work pretty much OK for most of us. After a while I started chatting to one of the navigators who introduced himself as Jim Churcher, from Tunbridge Wells in Kent. Physically he was my opposite. He was dark haired and a fair bit taller than me, but he was quietly spoken and seemed a thoroughly decent chap. We decided to give it a shot and see how we got on together. I'll tell you now, I could not have made a better choice had I stayed in the room all day and spoken to every navigator on the airfield. He turned out to be everything I could have ever hoped for in a crew member and navigator. He was stable, reliable, calm and resolute. Almost totally unflappable, he never let me down and was always very supportive. Having said all that, he did have one bad trait. Being taller than me and long of leg he had a tendency to stride about the airfield in what were to me, at a mere 5 foot 5 and being short of leg, great galumphing strides that would have done credit to a kangaroo on a mission. We never did seem to effect a compromise. Either I was struggling to keep up with him, or he was taking deliberately short baby steps to keep in step with me. It must have looked pretty amusing to any onlookers as we walked out to our plane.

On 7 October, the Flying Officer (F/O) Bertie Boulter and Sgt Jim Churcher team were allocated a Mk XX Mosquito 'G' George, for bomber familiarization. So they set about getting used to the plane, working as a crew, familiarizing themselves with 'their' airfield and its surroundings and all the things they would soon need to know for operational duties. For just over an hour and a half they worked at this, including a brief but useful fifteen minutes of instrument work for Bertie as they went through cloud. The next day a cross-country mission in a Mk IV, code letter Q, to 25,000 feet took them three hours and fifteen minutes, of which a further thirty minutes were logged on instruments. It also checked their ability to trust each other, work together and overcome defects in the plane's equipment.

Some way short of the halfway point of the exercise, the second stage of one of the two-stage superchargers fitted to one of the Mosquito's engines started cutting in and out of its own accord. There was nothing he could do about it. They soldiered on with the affected engine increasing and decreasing in power from time to time as if it had a mind of its own. Fortunately as the power was reduced for landing, the delinquent supercharger would no longer be required and the subsequent landing was uneventful. However, it did serve to remind them that as good as the Mosquito was, occasionally things could go wrong with even the best kit.

On 11 October, in a different plane, they had a less dramatic cross-country practice mission. Again its duration was three and a half hours, this time with a substantial two hours on the instruments. Obviously at high altitudes they were on oxygen. This system was located under their seats with the contents gauges positioned so that they could be seen as the crew prepared for take-off. They were of course always thoroughly checked by the crew chief or one of the ground crew during a thorough pre-flight inspection of the plane. Nonetheless, all crew members, however trustful of their team, always gave that particular piece of kit their own final check before they taxied out for take-off.

The only flight in the following two days was to take a Mk XX on a night-flying test (NFT). This was always the practice with the Mosquito squadrons at Wyton. Every plane going on an operation was air tested to check that all the night-flying instruments and kit were fully functioning for that same evening's raid. The 14th and 15th were devoted solely to night-flying sorties, and produced six hours and fifty minutes to add to the log-book. Two more NFTs were undertaken on the 16th and 18th and another 25,000 feet night-bombing exercise for three hours and ten minutes occupied most of the evening of the 18th. A further repeat of this NFT and a 25,000 foot sortie followed on the 19th, and then they were ready to go. In his log-book Bertie noted. 'Certified that I have on two occasions practiced abandoning Mosquito aircraft.' H.E. Boulter. 20.10.44. Little did he realize at the time that this would be very valuable training indeed.

They were now operational.

We were transferred to 128 Squadron and assigned to 'A' Flight. 'A' Flight commander was S/Ldr Ivor Broom. I remember meeting him and his navigator Tommy Broom (no relation) in his office when I reported in. He was sitting behind his desk with Tommy standing next to him. He looked at Tommy.

'So this is Eddie Boulter? What shall we call him Tommy? I think he should be called Bertie the Boy, he looks very young.'

Tommy nodded and that was it. From that day onwards, all the time I was in the RAF I was Bertie. Fortunately for me the 'boy' bit was quickly dropped as a matter of convenience by almost everyone except Ivor; he managed to give me the full title every time we met. Bertie Boulter was now an RAF bomber pilot.

The build-up for an evening operation was always pretty much the same. Each day's activities were dictated by the battle order, which was usually posted up by 9–9.30 every morning. This listed the crews chosen for that day's bombing operation; no other information was included.

The planning for the operation(s) began when Group Headquarters informed the squadron commander where the target was and the required time on target, which usually occurred shortly after midday. Unless we had been on ops the night before, we were expected to arrive at the crew room at 9 and then conduct an air test on the plane we were allocated for the raid. If we had been on a raid the night before, then another crew would conduct the air test for us.

Meanwhile the squadron CO and his navigation officer had planned their timing. Say for instance that the target was Berlin. Time on target 01.00 hours, take-off time would then be assumed 23.00 hours. Time anticipated at dispersal would then be 22.00 hours. Navigators' briefing would commence at 20.00 hours with the pilots joining them at 20.30 hours. Actual take-off time would depend on the wind conditions on the day and would be finally adjusted after the Met. [meteorological] briefing to correct time on target back to 01.00 hours.

As the operational meal would be at 18.30 hours we had some time to spare in the afternoon. Usually we would write letters, read the papers, spend some time in the Link trainer, or chat to the other crews as the clock ticked round towards half past six. The squadron meal usually comprised eggs, bacon and possibly sausage. Beans and greens were firmly avoided as it was a combination which could lead to extreme discomfort at 25,000 feet. After that it was pretty much a question of getting our own personal preparations completed, putting on our flying kit and heading to the briefing. After it was over we went by crew bus to collect our parachutes and then on to the dispersal pans. This was usually about an hour before take-off. A crew chief generally had several planes under his charge, but he was always around with the rest of the ground crew at start-up time. At Wyton at least, the regime always allowed for a relaxed build-up. There was inevitably something for the pilot and navigator to do, but rarely any panic to get it done and they all knew their start-up and take-off times well in advance. Crews' minds were always fully occupied during this period, but never over-stressed. It was planned that way to keep their minds off the flak and fighter activities that could well lie ahead, and generally it was a process that seemed to work for most of them.

When we got back to Wyton there was a similar pattern of activity that followed each raid. The planes were parked and handed back to the ground crew, who were then advised of any defects or damage. We then were transported back to the briefing room in the crew bus, where we were to be interrogated by the intelligence officer about the raid. Being part of the Pathfinder operation, all crews were always quizzed thoroughly about the target indicators. We were all given cups of tea and coffee, liberally laced with rum, while we were in the debrief. Meanwhile the photo records from the planes themselves were retrieved and hurried to the station photographic unit for processing and evaluation the following day. We then handed back our parachutes, took off the flying kit and headed to our air-crew breakfast and possibly the bar. The sergeants, mainly the navigators, went to the sergeants' mess, and the bulk of the pilots to the officers' mess.

There was always a bit of chatter going on about the target and our thoughts on what the photos would show. All the aircraft carried cameras to record bombing accuracy and results. We had to be on top of our flying at that time as the automatic cameras needed straight and level flight to operate correctly. An operational Mosquito probably weighed in at about 25,000 pounds as it taxied out for take-off. We had used a couple of thousand pounds of fuel getting there, so when a 23,000 pound plane loses its 4,000 pound bomb load in one hit, it leaps upwards quite spectacularly. At that point to get the photoreconnaissance shots needed we had to hold it steady and fly straight and level for about twenty seconds.

A green flash would show for the first photo, then we would hold the plane in position until we saw the second flash. At that point we knew we were free to go home. If conditions were right, the intelligence boffins could check your bomb burst compared to the markers. They were long days, and bed was a welcoming sight in the early hours of the morning, after we had enjoyed our aircrew breakfast of eggs, bacon and sausage. We had our first breakfast at 08.00 hours and our aircrew breakfast about 04.00 hours the next morning – a full twenty hours later.

CHAPTER FIVE

First Operations

Monday, 23 October was a pretty normal day for most people at RAF Wyton – normal, that is, for an operational bomber base in the middle of World War 2. For Bertie and Jim Churcher, however, it was different from everything that had gone before, the culmination of years of training and effort. It was to be their first operation over enemy territory. The weather was fine, and the forecast for later in the night would change very little.

Jim and I talked about it earlier. We knew, or at least we felt we were ready to go and the fact that we had recently been transferred from 1655 MTU to 128 squadron seemed to confirm that others thought that also. So on 23 October, when I got to the squadron office just after nine in the morning, our name was on the battle order. Tonight we would be the crew of one of the planes that took off for Germany; not one of the crews allocated to do an NFT, then left behind. We had mixed emotions. We were overjoyed to be part of the team at last, and we were excited and apprehensive in equal measure. Perhaps this apprehension was more in anticipation of the unknown than any fear of getting killed, crashing or being shot at. We knew the Mosquito was almost too fast to catch, we had the cover of night, and the plane had a track record of minimum casualties. On top of that, like all young and inexperienced aircrew we had that wonderful. 'It won't happen to me' mentality. But above all else there was the determination not to let your chums down. That covered your crew, your ground crew, your flight, the squadron and above all else the other aircrews who you flew with.

We had completed the NFT of KB443 before lunch. For Jim this had included checking that the Loran and Gee navigation aids and the Mk 14 bomb sight were to his liking. After our supper at 16.30 hours I headed back to my room to put on my flying boots that had been cleaned and polished earlier in the afternoon. This had become a ritual for me and I never went on an operation without clean, shiny boots. Like most of the chaps on operations I had my lucky talisman – wherever I went, it went. I never climbed aboard an aircraft without my little black elephant in my pocket. It also served to remind me to empty my pockets of any means of identification, in case of capture by the Germans. I removed my collar and tie and put on my favourite jumper, scarf and battledress top. Apart from my Mae West, helmet and chamois gloves I was now kitted out for flying.

Jim meantime had been checking out his maps and various other bits of navigational equipment, and like me was ready to go as 18.15 hours approached. He went in to the briefing first, along with his fellow navigators, and the pilots joined them about half an hour later. When I got into the room there was the squadron commander and Ivor Broom, my flight commander, together with Tommy Broom, his navigator. As well as the route to be flown, the briefing also covered known hot spots like AA [anti-aircraft] gun concentrations, fighter airfields and as many hazards that could be reasonably thought of. The met officer had the latest weather information collected by 1409 Met Flight, which was also based at RAF Wyton. This included general weather to be expected between Wyton and the target as well as the all-important wind speed and direction. Using the Gee set each navigator could 'fine tune' the estimated information provided by the met officer, and it usually gave them something to criticize on their return.

We sat and looked at the map on the wall. The target name above the dot at the end of the outbound route and the beginning of the return route was Wiesbaden, a large town just a few miles to the west of Frankfurt. It would be a round trip of just over 1,000 miles that would take us a little over three and a half hours. The armourers had loaded our allocated bombs and markers for the operation and the ground crew had taken one last look round their charges before handing them over to the aircrews. Our thoughts and emotions were still the same as they had been all day, except that by now perhaps the excitement level was starting to rise even further.

Once at the aircraft the crew chief handed the pilot a clipboard with MOD Form 700 attached to it. It contained all the official words, effectively passing the temporary custody of the plane to its pilot. Bertie's Form 700 stated that on 23 October 1944, Mk XXV Mosquito KB443 was in good shape and ready to be released to service to F/O H.E. Boulter. He would have signed for it knowing that in a few hours he would be handing it back to its rightful keepers, his ground crew.

Jim and I looked round the outside of the plane, making particularly sure that the pitot head cover was definitely removed prior to flight. We obviously looked at the wheels and tyres and other bits we could reach and see. However, as it was night time and the highest point on a Mosquito was 17 feet 6 inches above the parking apron, even Jim, with a few inches more in height than me, could barely see much more than the underside of the wings and fuselage. But aircrew were known to walk round the aircraft and pull and push at things as well as occasionally kick tyres, so who were we as the new boys on the squadron to change the routine? Besides that, it usefully occupied a few more minutes of the waiting time. So we walked knowingly round the Mossie, pulled and pushed a few things and kicked the tyres, nodded to each other and clambered aboard.

Once in the aircraft another set of routines came into play as the crew began preparing the aircraft and themselves for the forthcoming raid. It was the only time that the Mosquito cockpit was a bit chilly. They could not start the Merlin engines too early or they would overheat (about twelve to fifteen minutes in the summer months and a bit longer in the winter). The V12s were big, substantial engines and took a while to warm up from dead cold, but once the needle started moving up the gauge, the crews needed to be ready to roll fairly soon. Needless to say the cockpit heater, although a very efficient piece of kit, was totally unusable until the engines were warm and it could pull the warm engine-coolant into play. It did, however, mean the Mosquito crews could fly without donning sheepskin flying jackets or electrically heated flying suits. This they considered to be quite a bonus.

It is interesting to note at this point that Bertie had less than thirty hours', total experience of solo night flying when he opened the throttles on KB443 that autumn evening and headed down the runway towards Wiesbaden.

The operation must have gone totally to plan, as I remember so very little of it. We all had the same briefing and we were all equipped with top-class radios that had excellent reception and as such there was no confusion over start-up times or take-off times. My log-book shows a mere fifty minutes on instruments for the whole operation, leaving two hours and fifty minutes of visual flight. It must have been a clear night, or the bulk of the clouds were very high, or very low, I really don't remember. We were shot at, and it must have been by an 88mm radar-controlled gun. The shell bursts were very close and I went into a hard dive to port before re-covering our height and heading.

About this time our aircraft were being fitted with two radar receivers. One, called the 'boozer', was tuned in to the radar transmission from the German ground tracking stations. The Germans could detect both position and height from that and obviously direct both night fighters or normal ack-ack [anti-aircraft] guns in our direction. While this was happening, the 'boozer' glowed a dull red. German defences were divided into sections and the radar stations eventually had to hand the plot to the next section because of range limitations. To confuse the radar operators and make it harder for them to track us we could change height and/or direction. If this was un-successful then the process would be repeated until it hopefully took place near a change-over point for the Germans. When an 88mm radar-controlled gun locked on to the plane the 'boozer' light glowed bright red. The pilot waited twenty to twenty-five seconds, depending on his height, to ensure that the gun was fired and the shell was on its way. Then a quick change in heading by 30 to 40 degrees ensured that the plane was not around when the shell arrived and exploded.

The other radar system was Monica. This was tuned to the frequency employed by the airborne-interceptor radar fitted to the German night fighters. When this locked on, Monica glowed white and much weaving climbing, diving and rubber-necking went on while the crew tried to catch sight of the enemy. The vapour trails from the engines were also a concern for the crews while this was going on and changes of height were frequently tried to avoid them. The first night operations by the Boulter/Churcher crew were without the benefits of the 'boozer'or Monica receivers. Such was the call for them that we completed the first ten or twelve trips without the new systems as we waited our turn to have them fitted.

Monica also became activated in cirrus cloud by the electrical charge associated with the phenomenon of St Elmo's fire. Regardless of cause, any pilots ignored this white light at their peril. However the crews always felt that the speed of the Mosquito would put them out of reach of most of the pursuing fighters and generally they were right. The Mosquito could outrun an FW 190; the ME 410 was not quite so easy, and the ME 262 jet was impossible but it was scarce and had limited duration. The Mosquito being unarmed, it was indeed their only chance of survival.

You wanted to get to the target on time. Too late was bad enough, but too early meant that the TIs [target indicators] had not yet been dropped and to overshoot the target and do a 180 degree turn to head back to the target area from the opposite direction was fraught with danger. It was then necessary to execute another 180 degree turn to be at the right height, airspeed and heading for the bombing run; much better to get it right first time. Jim Churcher and I had worked that one out for ourselves, long before that first operation. The lead marker plane would advise by radio the time before or the time after zero hour, by calling out 'H minus one' or 'H plus one', for releasing the markers. At zero hour we were all pretty busy trying to drop our bombs on target and on time. Occasionally of course there were collisions and frequently there were near misses. You needed your wits about you, a sharp look-out and a good slice of luck. Like all German cities, Wiesbaden was heavily defended by anti-aircraft guns and searchlights though I really don't remember it overmuch. I cannot even recall talking about it with Jim, either on the way home or in the days that followed, although I presume we did.

We were on the battle order in the squadron office the next day. Jim and I thought this normal as we were on the squadron strength and needed the experience. When we arrived at the office about midday, another crew had completed our NFT for us. It was only when we saw the operations map as we sat down for the briefing that we realized that today was not going to be the same as yesterday. We were to bomb Hanover (a city I was to visit four times in all before the war's end). It was a slightly longer trip, a slightly different route and a different bomb load (four 500 pound bombs and no TIs). Take-off time was earlier than our first operation and my log-book shows only thirty minutes on instruments. The flight must have been clear all the way to the target as Wyton was completely fogged in on our return and we were diverted to Foulsham, a bomber base just to the north of the market town of Dereham in mid-Norfolk. The weather in Norfolk was not brilliant but at least it was adequate. We arrived there just after 10 o'clock. When we landed and taxied in we were met by a ground crew who looked after us like one of their own. They provided an intelligence officer to debrief us while the operation was fresh in our minds and then they whisked us over to the mess for some supper, a pint and eventually a room. The next morning we were given breakfast and took a leisurely twenty-five minute, low-level flight back to Wyton. We had a couple of days off after that.

On the 28th we were not on the battle order when I went to the squadron office in the morning to look. Jim and I were allocated KB387 for an NFT which according to my log-book took us all of fifteen minutes to complete. Jim and I had done nearly half a dozen of those air tests by now, so we pretty much had the routine off pat. Shortly after landing I was called back into the office and told to pick up an Oxford and fly a S/Ldr Young down to RAF Halton in Buckinghamshire. I had not been there before and the airfield notes implied it was a fairly small grass field. It had a north–south runway of just 1,000 yards. All the other cross runways were somewhat less than 700 yards apiece. I don't recall any problems so it must have been OK. It did surprise me to note that it had been less than six weeks since I last flew an Oxford. I was amazed how quickly the time had passed, and life had changed.

The following day, 29th, the Boulter/Churcher team's name was back on the order. They were allocated the familiar Mk XXV Mosquito KB 387 for a raid on Cologne. With no instrument time logged and no outstanding memories of the trip, it has to be assumed that it was as routine and uneventful as any bombing operation ever got. They were home by 9 o'clock and had plenty of time to head for the mess. The load had again been four 500 pounders. Thus Bertie's first month on operation with 128 Squadron drew to a close. He had added a mere twelve hours and fifty minutes to his log-book, but that had included three bombing raids deep into the heart of Germany. He felt that he was at last getting to grips with the enemy and doing the job he originally volunteered to do.

On a more domestic note, it has to be pointed out that on joining 128 Squadron, Bertie was allocated a room to share in the officers' mess with Tommy Broom. This in itself was rather a novel experience. Tommy was a slightly older character than most other aircrew members of the squadron, almost ten years older than Bertie. He was also a keen supporter of the social side of the officers' mess, at Wyton, (or any other group to which he had been attached, for that matter). He valued his drinking time such that it was rumoured that his accuracy of navigation was driven by the need not to waste time over enemy territory and get back to the mess bar without wasting a single second. Few who knew him would cast doubts on the accuracy of that statement.

CHAPTER SIX

November 1944

Days of the week and weeks of the month made little difference to the operational aircrew at Wyton or elsewhere within Bomber Command. Except when bad weather intervened, the RAF flew round the clock every day, seven days a week; there was simply no let up. By now the German war machine was starting to feel the pressure and Bomber Command was not about to ease off.

Jim and I were back in the familiar surroundings of KB 443 again. For the first time ever we had completed our own NFT in our own plane prior to the operation. However, this time when we sat down in the briefing room we were told that tonight we were hitting the Germans in their heart. We were heading for Berlin, and were allocated a take-off time of 17.14 hours. Of course the squadron had been there before on many occasions. In fact the soon to be legendry 'Flying Brooms' (Tommy and Ivor), later to become Air Marshal Sir Ivor Broom, KCB, CBE, DSO, DFC**, AFC, and S/Ldr Tommy Broom DFC**, had already been there on many occasions to make their mark. It was to take us five hours and five minutes to complete the trip, the longest single flight I had ever flown. When we got back I cannot ever remember being quite so tired. I felt totally wiped out, and it was not yet 10.30 in the evening.

It is sometimes forgotten that standard barometric

pressure is 14.7 pounds per square inch at sea level, but at our operational height it was just a fraction of this. Blood, which carries oxygen around the human body, tries to expand due to this reduced pressure. As the body cannot let this happen, every muscle surrounding veins and arteries is therefore tensed. Flying at some 25,000 feet in an unpressurized aircraft as we did, caused fatigue. Gas in the stomach and intestines also expands and can cause great discomfort, even pain, unless suitably vented – little wonder aircrew pre-op meals did not include greens or beans! The Mk XVI actually had a pressurization system for the cabin, but we never used it. It would have needed switching off to drop 'window' and would have been disastrous if the cabin was holed by flack; anyway it could not be switched on and off willy-nilly at altitude.

When you think our previous operational trips had all been under the four hours, this was a big step up for us new boys; even poor old Jim could not relax on the way home as he had both his navigational duties to carry out and his role as my second pair of eyes to detect the presence of night fighters to perform. Certainly we were confident that we could always out-run the fighters on the way home as now we were minus the bomb load and over half the fuel load. Nonetheless Jim always kept a very sharp look out all the way home.

The Boulter/Churcher team did an NFT for someone else the next day, but were not on the battle order. It was an easy day and it did give Bertie the opportunity to admire a Sunbeam 350 motorcycle one of the men was using as personal transport round the station. It would suit him admirably for popping home to Norwich the following week when he was due some leave. He had a preliminary chat with the Sunbeam's owner, during which it was established that it was quite possible that a deal could be arranged. It sounded hopeful but would have to wait, as work-wise the next few days were going to be hectic. Operations on 3, 4 and 6 November took them back to Berlin, to Hanover and to Gelsenkirchen, all in MM194. It also introduced them to another variant of the trusty Mosquito, the Mk XVI. Although it was very similar to the Mk XXV, Bertie had never even done an NFT in one of these variants prior to starting the take-off roll on the Berlin operation on the 3rd.

They were very similar, of course, in the cockpit layout and the position and feel of the controls; fortunately the handling was pretty much the same. The main operational difference with the Mk XVI was that it had increased torque from the 1,750 horse power Merlins, which required extra care on take-off. The ordnance was different in that that it carried a single 4,000 pound bomb. When you released it, the plane seemed to shoot up a couple of hundred feet. I'm sure it wasn't that much, but it seemed like it. It did put a bit more pressure on Jim and the other navigators though. With the Mk XXV you had four bombs and the knowledge that there was always a bit of a spread with them, so you always had four chances of getting it dead right, with the 4,000-pounder it had to be exactly right every time. Then there was Tommy Broom of course; as the senior and most experienced navigator, he was second to none in his job and his accuracy was legendary. All the navigators knew that and tried their hardest to be as good. Tommy of course was always willing to give much-needed advice and help to the fledgling navigators under his wing to help them along.

One of the minor problem we pilots encountered at about the same time was the over-lightness of the Mosquito's controls in roll. It was very easy to over-input on the ailerons and so significant was the problem to some of the pilots that the ground crew modified the planes by reducing the servo effect on the ailerons. That helped, but the real problem was actually in the pilot's head. When stars were visible on a clear night, the re-fraction made it appear that they were down on the right or left-hand side. If they appeared to be on the left it gave the pilot a strong feeling that the aircraft was banked to the right and that he should roll to the left. If you ignored that and put your head down in the cockpit and trusted the instruments you would be OK. Aero medicine at the time was coming to grips with vertigo.

The other problem we encountered with the Merlins on some of the Mosquitos was the tendency for the plugs to 'lead-up', causing misfiring and vibration, sometimes even the loss of an engine. Initially the engineering officer established that if you went into fine pitch every fifteen minutes or so, this could blow the lead out of the plugs. It was only a temporary solution and we pilots felt we already had enough to do on any raid, and hoped a more permanent solution would soon be found. The main cause was the high lead content of the aviation fuel we used. The second problem was the fact that the fuel mixture was heated in the superchargers and then travelled through the wing intercoolers before it went into the engine. The intercooler was obviously too effi-cient and the fuel was not hot enough when it reached the cylinders. Our crew chief could do nothing about the problem with the lead content of the fuel, but he could make the intercooler less efficient and make everything run hotter. It worked like a charm. The leading–up problem virtually went away and the remainder of the engine readings stayed satisfactory, though not before Rolls Royce suggested weakening the mixture, which gave the first pilot to try it on a fully loaded take-off an interesting experience.

The return trip to Berlin was a lot quicker than the previous operation. Whether MM194 (the Mk XVI) was quicker than KB443 (the Mk XXV), or whether the wind strength and direction played a part in it, is open to conjecture, but Bertie's log-book shows four hours and thirty-five minutes compared to the five hours plus of two days before. Hanover was three hours and twenty minutes and Gelsenkirchen was a mere three hours and ten minutes. Only the Hanover flight logged any instrument time.

The 8th and 9th were days of flying NFTs, both in KB443, before going to Norwich for a week's leave, to be taken with the recently acquired Sunbeam motorcycle.

Soon after taking ownership of the Sunbeam, I began to feel that there was a problem with the front forks and was not at all happy with the motorcycle's steering characteristics. I therefore took it to our flight hut and left it with our 'chiefy', who knew all about these things, to sort out. The following afternoon I gratefully collected this magnificent gleaming black and gold steed, now in full working order, and started the short journey round the perimeter track back to the officers' mess. I hadn't travelled very many yards when I came face to face with a Miles Messenger heading my way along the perimeter track. I turned to the left and onto the grass to allow it to pass, but it suddenly turned and taxied straight at me and my Sunbeam. At this stage I had dismounted and was trying to push the Motorcycle round the wing of the Messenger, which now stopped.

There was a short interval while the pilot, AVM Bennett, removed his flying helmet and donned his cap, adorned as it was with an alarming quantity of gold braid. Releasing the canopy, he stood up and beckoned me towards him. He enquired if I had had any instruction in airmanship, my name and squadron. When I had supplied answers to all three questions he proceeded to administer a most efficient dressing down. He was right of course: I should really have pulled to the right, on the side of the track away from the airfield instead of turning on to the active section as I had done. He then ordered me to report myself to the station commander for obstructing the passage of an aircraft on the perimeter track.

I reported to Group Captain 'Dixie' Dean DSO, DFC and explained what had happened. Dixie Dean in his previous life had been a builder; he was a practical man. He rummaged through his drawers and produced a scale rule. He then marked on the station plan on his wall the correct position of the Messenger and its scale size taken from a reference manual, and the scale size of the Sunbeam. He then stood back and looked at his handiwork. Quite solemnly he then turned to me and declared that in his opinion there was ample passing space, and now he had fully considered the matter I should return to the mess and forget about it.

A few weeks later on a Sunday afternoon S/Ldr Ivor Broom found me and announced that he and I were invited to AVM Bennett's house to take afternoon tea. As a relatively new 'sprog' officer I naturally felt overawed to be taking tea with the great man himself, three group captains and Ivor, and to find myself included in the light-hearted conversation. Don Bennett's wife Ly served us tea and I felt both very honoured, spoilt and very puzzled. I then began to realize that although Don Bennett had an extremely tough job to do, under that stern exterior there was a man with a big heart.

The journey between Wyton and Norwich along the roads of Cambridgeshire and Norfolk were great fun, but bitterly cold. However much I wrapped up and encased myself in layers of clothes, including my flying kit, I always arrived home extremely cold, particularly my hands and feet. On those journeys I remembered fondly the wonderful heater in the dear old Mossies. It was also not unusual to be plastered with mud and road grime when I got home or back to Wyton, just to add to the discomfort. The roads round the airfield were notoriously narrow and always appeared to be awash with mud. The main traffic seemed to be fuel tankers constantly bringing in the fuel needed to keep the squadrons operational. Inevitably they met head on and demolished the grass verges as they squeezed past each other, leaving the carriageway inches deep in mud – not the best surface for an inexperienced motorcyclist to encounter.

The first time I fell off the Sunbeam I was in Norwich. My old friend from Theodore, Harald Mercer, and I met up for some leave together. He was now a flight lieutenant in the Canadian Air Force, flying Wellingtons on a Canadian squadron based up in Yorkshire. One icy day we headed up the Dereham road with me at the controls and Harald on the pillion seat. Turning off onto a side road, the Sunbeam decided that it had had enough and deposited Harald and me unceremoniously on our rear ends on the tarmac as it departed on its side towards Dereham. We were more or less unhurt from the incident, but it did remind me that I could come to more harm having fun in Norwich than I could while dropping bombs from 25,000 feet over Berlin.

I sold the Sunbeam in Norwich on my next leave home, putting an end to my short-lived motorcycling career, and moved on to the relative safety of four wheels. I acquired a Ford Eight, and it was a real beauty. It went well, it looked smart and it was totally and utterly reliable. Unfortunately as I parked it outside a shop in Norwich one day, the shopkeeper offered me double what I had paid for it a couple of months earlier. To me that was a deal I could not pass up, and the Ford and I parted company. Armed with the cash I headed off to look for another mode of transport and contemplated a rosy future after the war in the motor trade. I bought another Ford Eight for the same price as I paid for the first one, but this one was a real dog. Over the next few weeks I parted with every penny of my profit getting the new car to perform as well as its predecessor. Eventually it did, and it served me well until a Singer Le Mans sports car took my fancy. That too ate money to keep running but I persevered with it until the war's end. However the relentless parting of the cash on the upkeep of my chosen cars put paid to my dream of becoming a motor trader. Perhaps it was for the best after all.

Prior to joining 128 Squadron Bertie had amassed just eighteen hours' solo night flying on a single-engined plane and twenty-nine and a half hours on multi-engined aircraft, of which just over fifteen hours had been on Mosquitos. It was armed with that experience and a signed declaration in his log-book that he had twice practised the escape procedure for the Mosquito aircraft, that he had lined up on Wyton's runway for his first ever night operation over Germany in the last week in October; now by the second week in November he had virtually doubled that logged time. Fortunately he took to night flying in the Mosquito very easily.

You got used to life on a squadron, rather than what you were actually doing. Every raid was different in some way or other. Sometimes you seemed to be very busy all the while, other times it was much easier, though all the time you were acutely aware that every German city was ringed with anti-aircraft guns and searchlights. We were told at the briefing if we were on the main raid or a 'spoof'. If we were the first wave of the main raid then we knew that the heavies would have taken off before us so that they would arrive over the target a few minutes after us to bomb on the target indicators. As we were at different heights it was not unusual to see no one going out or on the return. That was how we liked it. When we did see someone else it was usually time to take avoiding action. Unless it was a bright moonlit night, the first indication that you were close to another plane was the turbulence created by its props. Then you knew it was close. You immediately pushed on the stick, throttled back and hopefully swept underneath him. It was only then that you saw the blue flames from his exhausts and certainly the underside of the plane, or the silhouette against the sky, if the night was clear.

There were other dangers we just hadn't thought of at all. I recall that it was about this time that poor old Jim actually got hit. Piecing it together later, it appeared we ran into some shrapnel from a shell burst above and ahead. However when a Mosquito hit pieces of shrapnel at 300 miles an hour plus, they had no bother piercing the fuselage of the plane and hitting whatever was inside. In this case it was Jim. He quietly said to me 'I've been hit in the left shoulder', then immediately began feeling about under his kit to assess the damage. After a fairly short while he told me he could find no blood or hole. He also chose that time to give me a fresh heading to steer to get us home! At that point I was greatly relieved to realize that whatever had happened, Jim was going to live. He had an enormous black bruise covering a large area of chest and upper arm, which he sported for days. But other than being mightily sore and tender he was thankfully OK. As far as we could tell the flak fragment hit the webbing of his safety straps and chute harness and that, added to the thickness of the rest of his flying kit, saved him further damage. It was a bit close all the same. Later we found the piece of shrapnel. It was about 2 inches long and just over ½ inch square. Jim kept it as a souvenir.

On 18 November a three and a half hour round trip took them to the huge synthetic fuel plant at Wanne-Eikel, just ten minutes beyond the Dutch border near Venlo, with a bomb load of four 500-pounders. There was some cloud on the way, and for an hour they flew on instruments. Not surprisingly they were home well before 10 o'clock.

Their next operation to Sterkrade was very similar, both in timing and bomb load. However the trip to Nuremburg in MM410, another Mk XVI, was a totally different story.

MM410 was a new plane to us, though similar in every respect to all the other Mk XVIs that we had flown. It was a 'spoof' or diversionary raid to Nuremburg that night, with the main bomber force heading for Munich. Because of this we seemed to have more 'window' than usual stored in the bomb-aiming position that Jim would occupy later in the trip. We wanted to fool the Germans into thinking there were more of us than there really were and that we were the main raid. Hopefully the *Luftwaffe* fighter controllers would send the fighters up from a wide area, to give us a hard time. This would then necessitate the fighters returning to base to refuel and possibly rearm, just as the heavies came in to start their bombing runs on the main target. We believed that the German night fighters only had about fifty minutes' duration with the throttles fully open trying to find us and they would need to refuel before the heavies arrived over Munich. That night I'm sure Jim was convinced that our ground crew had thought there were more than the two of us in the plane for that trip to help the bundles of 'window' anti-radar foil through the chute. It seemed to take him forever to get rid of it, but he had no choice, as he needed the space to get to the bomb sight and release our 4,000 pound bomb.

The bomb run went OK, we held steady after the bomb release and were rewarded with the camera flashes to record the accuracy of our efforts. I turned on to the heading Jim gave me for our return home and settled down for the flight back to Wyton. After just ten minutes I noticed that the starboard engine was showing signs of running hotter than before. I watched it closely as the coolant temperature climbed up the scale while at the same time the oil pressure reading was falling back towards the zero end of its scale. I was about to tell Jim, but he made it obvious that the situation in the engine department had already grabbed his full and undivided attention. When the coolant got hot enough and the oil pressure low enough, I shut down the engine, feathered the prop and trimmed the rudder and aileron to lift the wing by about 4 or 5 degrees to compensate. I remember saying to Jim, it was not a problem as these things were almost as good on one engine as they were on two. He nodded, though I'm not sure he was totally convinced. We lost about 40 knots in speed, but could maintain height.

That was until a further fifteen or so minutes passed when the gauges of the port engine started to copy those of its now silent companion. I unfeathered the prop of the starboard engine and was pleased to notice that the oil and coolant gauges were back nearer to where they should have been. I then feathered the port prop and shut that engine down. Jim and I looked at each other and nodded agreement to the instant plan to attempt to get the plane home if at all possible. A crash landing was not a sensible option at night and abandoning the plane while it was still capable of flying seemed a daft idea. There was just the Channel to worry about – if we got that far.

Needless to say the gauges did not stay in their safety zones for long. The port engine was shut down and feathered, and was hopefully cooling down at the same rate as the starboard one had earlier. Jim had been working hard replotting our route and speeds and had announced when we were back over Allied-held territory, which was a small step in the right direction; then as I refired the port engine he announced that we were over France, at least as far as he could tell. We could see nothing, but as his navigation was always spot on I would have put money (as well as my life) on his accuracy. The time intervals of the stop, start, stop, restart sequence was getting shorter and shorter as we lost height and the outside air temperature rose. We were now approaching the Channel coast and were in radio contact with RAF Manston, who in their usual cheery, supportive manner gave us an optimistic interpretation of our situation, urged us to keep going and advised us that we only had 10 miles to the Kent coast. Jim knew better and quickly confirmed to me we were much nearer Dunkirk than Dover.

By then we had used up over 17,000 feet and were getting close to decision time. Now we were swapping engines every few minutes as the warmer air at lower levels failed to cool them as well as the colder air had at 25,000 feet. Crossing the Channel was beginning to look less and less of an option. Manston had just given us their latest press-on briefing when the engines made the decision for us. Both oil pressure gauges dropped below zero and both coolant gauges hit their top stops. Our Merlins had no coolant and no lubrication and we were now down to 7,000 feet. It was the end of the line; Rolls Royce designs were good, but not so good that they could run without either vital fluid. Flames emerged from the engine nacelles and streamed back from the wings for 40 or so feet from the pods. They had had enough and were about to let go. The cockpit was now full of smoke, so using the intercom – which was fortunately still working – Jim and I agreed that we both thought it was time to leave. We were now at 7,000 feet.

I advised Manston that we were baling out and gave them a long count to twenty to make quite sure they got a good fix on our position. By then Jim had jettisoned the bottom hatch and was already halfway out. I remembered that in training we were taught to locate and grip the parachute 'D' ring before we jumped. Jim had also remembered the 'D' ring training. Unfortunately being a bit bigger than me he had hit his elbow as he scrambled through the hatch, which in turn had jerked his hand enough to pull the 'D' ring and activate the 'chute. When I looked at the hatch I could see from the glow from the cockpit lights, which were fortunately still working, that he was half in and half out with the 'chute starting to billow. Thinking probably more of myself than him at the time, I gave his right shoulder a hefty kick downwards and he popped out of the hatch like the proverbial cork from a bottle. I had trimmed the plane as best I could, but a Mosquito without power descended like a brick. That probably had not helped Jim in his efforts to clear the hatch; as I scrabbled through after him into the darkness I remembered that I had left my officer's cap tucked behind the seat. I didn't give it another thought; it would have to stay with the plane.

The Mossie's glide speed with both engines out was about 180–200 knots. As I exited the hatch I counted to three as quickly as I dared before pulling my 'D' ring. The physical forces involved when the 'chute snapped open therefore gave a hefty retardation to my forward velocity, which at the time was somewhat greater than my speed of descent. We were told in training that this initial deceleration was virtually all transmitted through the crutch straps of the harness and that it was important to have them fully tightened. The sudden deceleration certainly helped to take my mind off our immediate problems. When the tears eventually cleared from my eyes I was able to work out that I was still floating above a thin layer of broken stratocumulus, and as yet the ground was not really visible even in the bright moonlight. But what I could see eventually appeared to be a landscape scattered with silver discs. For a while I could not work out what they were. My mind started to question what I was seeing. It hardly resembled any land that I was familiar with. It was certainly not the sea, and anyway Jim had insisted that we were still over France, however near to the coast we were. I had been looking round for Jim, but saw nothing, and of course common sense dictated that he would be at least a mile or two away from me because of the natural time delay in my departing the aircraft. As I drifted closer to the ground it eventually became clear that these mysterious silver discs were in fact shell holes filled with water from the recent heavy rains in the area.

I hit the ground with a pretty hard but squelchy thud. I was in France. I glanced at my watch; it was just after 4 o'clock in the morning, I would obviously not be getting to bed just yet. As I stood there trying to gather my wits, I heard what sounded to me like a couple of rounds from some sort of field gun. I then started to have doubts about where I was. Before we jumped, Jim had estimated we were somewhere in the Dunkirk area; I was now not quite so sure. Training kicked in and I bundled up my 'chute and buried it in a shell hole, then covered it with a layer of dirt. I found my way out of the field and headed off down the road. It was not long after this that I realized I no longer had my small escape kit with me. In my haste I must have buried it with the 'chute – so much for training! There was no way I was going back for it, even if I could have found it in the mud and darkness; I would have to survive without it. A little later, as I trudged on, the cloud thinned and broke in places sufficient for me to see some of the Great Bear and Polaris and work out that at the next road junction a south-westerly direction would seem to suit me best. It was now 5 o'clock.

Although the road started taking me more to the south, it still seemed the best route. So far I had seen no one, friend, foe or local; the place seemed deserted. Even a field with some guns in it seemed abandoned – until I heard the command 'Fire', immediately followed by two guns roaring out in quick succession. Then my mind raced. Was that 'Fire' in English or *'Feuer'* in German? Certainly it sounded like an English word, but somehow it seemed to have a foreign accent. I stood still and strained my ears for any further words to give me a clue as to the nationality of the gun battery. Silence reigned. Thinking traditional thoughts of discretion and valour, I moved away from the area as quickly and quietly as I could. The next road junction soon appeared and gave me an option to proceed back in the south-westerly direction I felt provided me with the best chance of meeting up with Allied troops. It was a narrower road and soon led me to a small row of cottages. They were derelict, but as I found out, not unoccupied. The word 'Halt' rang out some distance in front of me, but I knew it was not directed at me.

Now was that 'Halt' or was it *'Halten'*? Somehow, as before, it did not sound 'fully' English. Once again no further words followed, so the nationality of the speaker could not be positively identified; or was I getting paranoid? The sentry was saving his breath, stamping his feet in the cold and banging his hands together and coughing, but not a further word did he utter. It was most unhelpful. I went behind the derelict cottages and crept towards the spot from which the noises were originating to see if I could identify him. I couldn't, it was still too dark to see, so again I thought it better to push on and quietly retreated away from the area. I was getting good at doing that. I went back to the fork in the road and headed on south again.

I came to a gentle right-hand bend which seemed to be leading me towards a very small village. By now dawn was just breaking and I could make out a line of tracked vehicles parked on the right-hand side of the road. As I came closer I could see that they were indeed tanks – but whose? There were eight or ten of them all parked close together but there appeared to be no markings on them, or at least none that I could see. When I reached the head of the column I squeezed close to the hedge to took a look round the hidden side of the lead vehicle. In the dim light of early morning I could still see no identification markings on them at all. It was as quiet as the proverbial grave. Whoever they belonged to, one thing was certain; their crews were not around, or if they were then they were all asleep, including any sentries that had been posted. I particularly remember looking for anything that might have identified them as German – a really strange thing to do, as that was the last thing I wanted to see. As a positive identity was not possible, I headed past them into what was then unknown territory. Again my mind was racing. If they were German, should I go back or should I carry on? If indeed they were English or American was I moving towards friendly troops, or away from them? As I could answer none of these questions, however many times I asked myself and however many times I rephrased them in my mind, I decided that the best thing to do was to carry on.

A couple of miles further on I came to a farmyard and farmhouse on my right; I could now see quite well as it was almost light. There was a dim light shining through a slit at the bottom of one of the shuttered windows. Plucking up all my courage and rehearsing my best schoolboy Canadian French I peered through the crack to see the farmer getting dressed ready to start the day. I tapped on the shutter. *'Ici Anglais . . . .RAF . . . Ouvrez la porte, s'il vous plait.'* At least that's what it sounded like to me, though I'm not sure that it did to him. The farmer, needless to say was more than a mite surprised to hear a disemboided voice that early in the morning, coming through his bedroom window as he struggled, hopping up and down on one foot, to get his legs into his trousers. He opened the door and let me in. We conversed sufficiently well to make him understand I needed to contact the nearest English soldiers and for him to let me understand that they were indeed in the vicinity and resting up in an old mill building a little further down the road, in the direction I had been heading.

I wandered into the mill to meet up with a bunch of squaddies standing and sitting round having their first brew–up of the day. In no time I was clutching a hot steaming mug myself; it tasted great. I had some breakfast with them and stayed there until a young lieutenant arrived in a jeep-like vehicle to take charge of me. I had two priorities; first to find Jim Churcher and then to get a message back to Wyton to let the squadron know where I was (in fact I was in the rural district outside Dunkirk, Jim's navigation had, as usual, been absolutely spot on). During the chat I told the young lieutenant of my walk and my accent identification problems. It obviously amused him quite a bit and he smiled as he explained that the Germans still held Dunkirk, but were completely surrounded and contained by an independent unit from the Czech army, hence the use of English and yet the strange 'foreign' accent. It was obvious really when it was explained to me, but not quite so obvious just an hour after abandoning the warm, familiar surroundings of my Mosquito. We found Jim just before 11 o'clock. It was he whom I had heard being challenged by the Czech sentry a few hours earlier. Once identified, he had been taken to their officers' mess and entertained in a very hospitable way. Even after a few hours' sleep, we still had a somewhat inebriated sergeant on our hands.

Later that same afternoon our young army escort drove us to the Dunkirk beaches and showed us how the retreating Germans had booby-trapped their pill boxes and bunkers with wires, trigger devices, explosives and hand grenades. Some of the grenades were rigged to explode the moment the safety pin was pulled. We were very lucky to have such a knowledgeable chap with us. For the uninformed like us, death lurked in every discarded box and through every door. Our loathing for the Germans was given quite a boost after seeing for ourselves how determined they were, even in retreat, to kill anybody on our side. By five that evening we were on our way to Ostend in an armoured car. By peeking out of the narrow slits in its body we were able to see the shattered countryside slip past. It was a sobering sight. We were soon allocated beds for the night, fed, and advised to get our heads down early as we were on the first boat out in the morning.

That boat turned out to be an MTB [Motor Torpedo Boat] and we cleared the harbour entrance before first light. It was 5 a.m. as we headed out into the Channel for a very rapid trip back to Dover.

Dockside Dover reintroduced us to British bureaucracy. We were sent into a little room with a little man sitting behind a little desk. His job, he explained was to interview all aircrew returning to England. I seem to recall he was a pilot officer or flying officer, and he looked a typical 'wingless wonder' to me. I explained the circumstances of our adventures and he seemed satisfied. He then started questioning Jim. Whether it was because Jim was a sergeant, I'll never know, but he started to give him a really hard time. He began asking him what I thought were stupid questions about London theatres. What shows did he see, did he go up to London to see shows when he was on leave, that sort of thing. It was at that point that I lost it. It wasn't easy for me at a mere 5 foot 5¼ inches tall to reach over and grab his lapels, but I did. I then explained to him, probably in a rather terse, steely voice, how stupid I thought his questions were, and that all Jim and I needed were rail passes to Huntingdon, money for subsistence and he could phone Wyton or PFF [Pathfinder Force] HQ in Huntingdon if he needed any further information or wished to register a complaint about my behaviour. I believe at that point the penny must have dropped and he suddenly became quite helpful.

The young lieutenant in France had been swift off the mark getting through to Wyton and advising them that Bertie and Jim were safe and well; but it was not quick enough to prevent the first regulation telegram being sent back to Norwich and Tunbridge Wells advising their families that their sons had failed to return from their overnight operation.

This was the standard method used to pass on this bad news. However, the second telegram followed within the next twelve hours, advising the families that all was well and that the crew of Mosquito MM 410 was in fact now confirmed safe and well and back in England. The relief they must have felt can only be imagined. Bertie and Jim had a week's leave, and then it was December.

CHAPTER SEVEN

December 1944

An NFT of twenty minutes, actually undertaken at night, in a Mk XVI, PF441 on 2 December, started Bertie and Jim's month's operational flying as the cold of winter started to blow across the runways at Wyton. It was the first NFT they had been asked to fly at night, and strangely enough it would be the only one Bertie ever flew during the war. The following day they had a forty-five minute practice sortie reacquainting themselves with formation flying (in daylight of course) aboard PF401. The following day they were allocated its sister ship PF402 for the raid to Hagen, an industrial town in the Ruhr complex just south of Dortmund. This was another early start, with a take-off time of 17.56 hours. With just three hours and fifteen minutes logged it was the second shortest mission they would ever fly together. By 21.09 hours they were back at Wyton and parked up. By 22.30 hours they were happily propping up the bar in the mess.

We then did a couple of raids on Berlin, one after the other, albeit with a few days between them. On the 6th we took MM204 and on the 9th we were allocated PF411. Both were Mk XVIs and on both occasions we were armed with one 4,000 pounder. Both operations took four and a quarter hours from wheels up to wheels down, and on each occasion I spent almost two and a half hours on instruments, relying on Jim's usual spot-on navigation. I remember that the trip on the 9th was a bit

of a long one, we only started out at about 18.45 hours
and didn't get back until just after midnight. We then got
the following day completely clear of duties, we did not
even get an NFT and I seem to remember we managed
an extra hour or two in bed. Then it was a shortish
operation on the eleventh in PF412 on a daylight raid on
Hamborn. That was a distinct change for us – three and
a quarter hours and clear all the way according to my
log. It was quite a revelation to actually be able to see
where we were going, what we were doing and the
countryside beneath us. At 24,000 feet we could see
the troop concentrations and supply columns winding
their way inland towards the front line. It was also a rare
experience for Jim actually to see what he was aiming at.

The following day they were back on nights and destined
to go to Osnabruck. Bertie's log book indicates an hour of
instruments in an operation of three and a half hours. Again
they carried their usual load of a single 4,000 pound bomb.
This was in MM 204, a Mk XVI that would be their plane for
the best part of a week. This would be their longest association with any one aircraft in their entire operational time with
128 Squadron. (Bertie would top this later at 163 Squadron
with a remarkable association with KB 403, a Mk XXV that he
would fly on eighteen operations and at least seventeen other
non-operational occasions, during a period of just over ten
weeks.) The operation scheduled for the 16th was cancelled
after they had got airborne and reached their *en route* cruise
height. A radio call came through telling them the operation
was off and the bomb was jettisoned before they returned to
base. They were not too pleased. (Tommy Broom's good
friend Roy Ralston had once described the Mosquito's take-
off characteristics as 'un-handy' when fully fuelled and with
a 4,000 pound bomb in the belly. Thus aborted raids were not
appreciated by the crews after all the concentration and effort
of getting airborne.) However, someone obviously knew best
and they turned back. Their instructions were to keep their

drop tanks and not jettison fuel, so a really smooth and careful landing was still required. Even without the bomb an almost fully loaded Mosquito with drop tanks commanded great respect. The procedure for jettisoning bombs was well established. They flew out towards the North Sea, just to the north of Ipswich, and coasted out south of Orford Ness, over the Havergate Marshes, and then headed east to release their bomb loads some 30–35 miles offshore. The exact location was 5200N 0235E, easily fixed by using the Gee set on the aircraft. Bertie would visit this area several times before the war's end.

Duisburg, close to the Belgian border crossing at Venlo was our target for the night of the 16th. Well actually it was the early morning of the seventeenth to be precise. We had a take-off time allocated at 03.59 hours. That was about the worst time of day for me, as it was such an early start or late finish, depending on how you looked at these things. I guess I did not sleep too well or at least for too long. I remember feeling pretty washed out. This tiredness was to have much greater repercussions later. We took almost four hours to complete that op and I noted in my log that one and a half hours were spent on the instruments.

We drew operational duties again the next night. The Boulter/Churcher/MM204 team were off to Munster. Well, at least that's what was supposed to have happened. Needless to say it didn't. Whether from tiredness, lack of concentration or a combination of both factors, I got it wrong. Soon after take-off I hit a drem light post. [Drem lights marked the airfield circuit for the returning aircraft.] The drem lights of Wyton, Warboys and Upwood all intersected each other at various points, as the airfields were so close together. Loaded with the 4,000 pounder you needed speed rather than height at take-off, I can only assume I paid far too much attention to gaining that speed rather than gaining a couple of feet extra height at the time. The post smashed the clear view panel in the nose and we collected a reasonable length of power cable that cut into the starboard wing. There was a 140 knot gale blowing through the cockpit, together with an amazing amount of paper, dust and debris, all whirling about making life even more difficult than need be for a while. Then as we climbed to 8,000 feet the gale increased and it got a lot colder as we settled into our cruise speed.

We had a rather pressing problem on our hands and the city of Munster had just got lucky due to my lack of attention to detail. Again we flew towards Orford Ness with the calm voice of Jim Churcher reading out the headings from the Gee system that we needed to reach the jettison area. As we ran in towards the area we climbed to the prescribed height of 8,000 feet to jettison our bomb load. We felt the jump as MM204 lost her bomb and I heard Jim quietly giving me the steer back to land and to the emergency runway at Woodbridge. We would not be getting back home to Wyton. We stayed at Woodbridge for the next day as fog enclosed most of the East Anglia coast for the next twenty-four hours. I remember asking the ground crew at Woodbridge to check the trim systems and particularly the trim tab indicator systems. The crew chief came back and told me they were all working perfectly, but I had dented the spinner on the starboard engine. That was really the final confirmation that I needed, that this one was down to me, totally.

The day following that an Airspeed Oxford arrived from Wyton to collect us. MM204 would need a good bit of repair work before it went back into squadron service again. Jim and I had been lucky. I was annoyed with myself and Jim was understandably a little terse with me. I remember we went to the cinema in Woodbridge that evening. Jim was obviously still a bit peeved with me as he refused to walk slowly so that I

The official RAF photograph.

The Boulter family, taken in Theodore in the early 1930s.

Childhood days in Theodore were pretty good, even in winter. Here Bertie poses with Uncle Louis Peterson, a couple of chums and Peggy, his pony.

Moncton, Canada. With winter temperatures below -10°F it really was sometimes as bleak as it looked. Bertie passed through here heading to America for pilot training and again heading home.

Turner Field, Georgia, – 'Tent City'. Getting acclimatized to the temperatures and weather in the deep south of America, awaiting primary training. After Moncton just a day or two earlier it was quite a shock.

Moncton. With other intake cadets, posing for the classic 'spoof' shot. Cadets with kit issued, but not one of them having logged a single minute of their pilot training!

With training taking up most of his time in America, the odd moments of relaxation were greatly sought after and enjoyed. Doing nothing was a welcome respite.

Graduation ~~Program~~ Class 42-J

November 10th   *1942*

9:00 A.M.

AMERICAN AVIATION CADETS
will receive oath of office
as Second Lieutenants in the Army Air Forces
at the Flag Pole Presentation of Warrants
as Staff Sergeant Pilot to American Enlisted Students

9:30 A.M.

Newly Commissioned Second Lieutenants and Flying Sergeants
will take seats in the Post Chapel

9:45 A.M.

UNITED KINGDOM CADETS
will assemble in the Cadet Area and march to Post Chapel

10:00 A.M.

Invocation	*Chaplain Cuddy*
Address	*Ft. Lt. H. E. Taggart*
Congratulatory Address	*Col. James L. Daniel, Jr.*
Presentation of Diplomas	*Col. James L. Daniel, Jr.*
Presentation of Wings	*Major Charles G. Simpson, Jr.*
Benediction	*Chaplain Cuddy*

The programme of the graduation ceremony for Class 42 J on 10 November 1942,
Napier Field, Alabama.

Also presented on 10 November 1942, Bertie's Blind Flight Certificate; many further hours of instrument flying training were to follow before he flew a Mosquito on a bombing operation.

Blind Flight

SOUTHEAST AIR CORPS TRAINING CENTER
NAPIER FIELD, ALABAMA

This is to Certify that embryo Pilot _Boulter, Herbert E._ has satisfactorily completed a course of Instrument flying, on this _10_ Day of _November_ 19_42_, in "The Jeep" without Peeping.

INSTRUMENT OFFICER

United States Army

Army Air Forces

Be it known that
UK CADET HERBERT EDWARD BOULTER
has satisfactorily completed the course of instruction
prescribed for
PILOT TRAINING
at the ARMY AIR FORCES ADVANCED FLYING School.
In testimony whereof and by virtue of vested authority
I do confer upon him this

DIPLOMA

Given at NAPIER FIELD, ALABAMA this TENTH day
of NOVEMBER in the year of our Lord one thousand
nine hundred and FORTY-TWO.

JAMES L. DANIEL, JR.,
Colonel, Air Corps,
Commanding.

Attest

HERMAN L. HARRIS,
Major, Air Corps,
Adjutant.

U. S. GOVERNMENT PRINTING OFFICE : 1942—O—449500

Issued on 10 November at Napier Field, Alabama, Bertie's diploma from the United States Army Air Force, confirming that he had successfully passed the course of instruction prescribed for pilot training. From that day on he was a pilot.

A couple of hours prior to take-off and the 4,000 pounders are being loaded aboard ready for their one-way trip to Germany. Wyton, November 1944.

128 Squadron Mosquitos at Wyton taxiing out for a raid..

Heading off into the setting sun. For Bertie on nineteen occasions the destination would be Berlin.

The hatch into and out of the MkIII Mosquito cockpit.

Tail up and off to work. The first pilot would take the right-hand side of the runway, the second would take the left and so on. Generally it worked and they kept out of each other's way, but occasionally it got a bit close.

163 Squadron. The formal RAF photograph. Taken in March 1945, virtually all the aircrew survived the war.

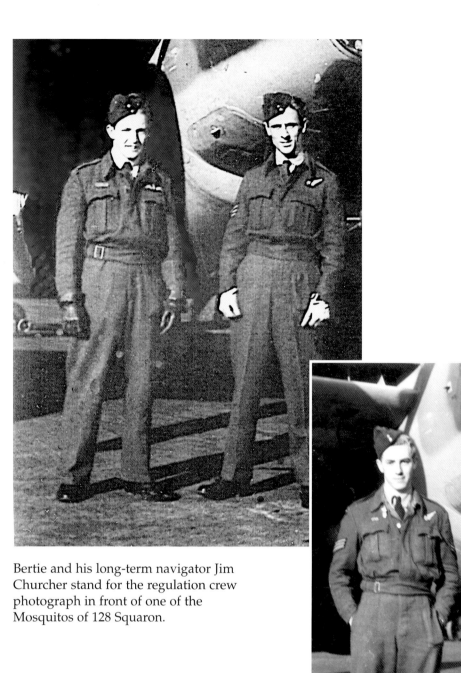

Bertie and his long-term navigator Jim
Churcher stand for the regulation crew
photograph in front of one of the
Mosquitos of 128 Squaron.

Chris Hart was the second of Bertie's
wartime navigators. As dependable as Jim
Churcher before him, with Chris, Bertie
was lucky to get a great crew mate and a
good solid navigator to fly with.

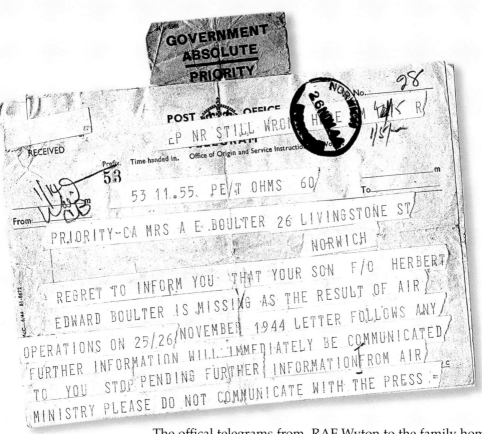

POST OFFICE TELEGRAM

EP NR STILL WRONG

RECEIVED

Prefix. Time handed in. Office of Origin and Service Instructions

53   53 11.55. PE/T OHMS 60/   To

From

PRIORITY-CA MRS A E BOULTER 26 LIVINGSTONE ST
NORWICH

REGRET TO INFORM YOU THAT YOUR SON F/O HERBERT
EDWARD BOULTER IS MISSING AS THE RESULT OF AIR
OPERATIONS ON 25/26 NOVEMBER 1944 LETTER FOLLOWS ANY
FURTHER INFORMATION WILL IMMEDIATELY BE COMMUNICATED
TO YOU STOP PENDING FURTHER INFORMATION FROM AIR
MINISTRY PLEASE DO NOT COMMUNICATE WITH THE PRESS =

The offical telegrams from RAF Wyton to the family home in
Norwich, the first announcing the bad news that Bertie and
Jim were missing, the second proclaiming that he was safe
and well in France.

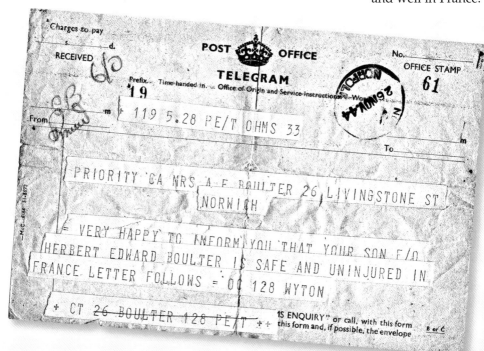

Charges to pay

s.   d.

RECEIVED

POST OFFICE

TELEGRAM   OFFICE STAMP

Prefix   Time handed in.   Office of Origin and Service Instructions   61
19

From   119 5.28 PE/T OHMS 33   To

PRIORITY CA MRS A E BOULTER 26 LIVINGSTONE ST
NORWICH

= VERY HAPPY TO INFORM YOU THAT YOUR SON F/O
HERBERT EDWARD BOULTER IS SAFE AND UNINJURED IN
FRANCE LETTER FOLLOWS = OC 128 WYTON

+ CT 26 BOULTER 128 PE/T ++   1S ENQUIRY" or call, with this form
this form and, if possible, the envelope   B or C

Berlin under attack towards the end of the war, shot from a Mosquito in Bertie's squadron.

128
AND
163
SQUADRONS
SAY

3RD.
JUNE
1945

"DOWN
UNDER"

WYTON

AU REVOIR AUSTRALIANS

At war's end, the Australian and New Zealand air crews were keen to go home, but not without the traditional RAF party. This was Bertie's card of the evening…

…duly signed by all on the rear of the illustration, 3 June 1945.

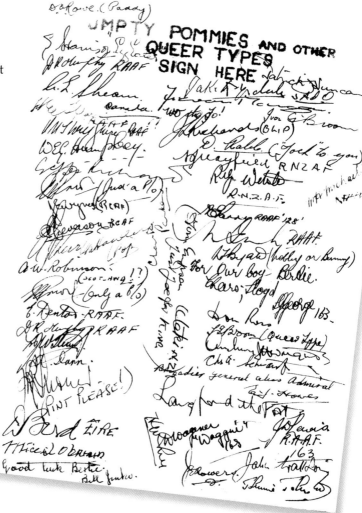

At Wyton effigies of Hitler, Mussolini and Emperor Hirohito form the backdrop to the early VE day celebrations. Later in the day they graced the huge celebratory bonfire. Bertie is sitting front row, second from the left, Tommy Broom third from right complete with trademark pipe.

24. Bertie and Flight Sergeant Derek Spinks, his peacetime navigator. Again in Bertie's view, a super crew member and a very competent navigator.

Bertie and Christine's wedding day, 31 January 1952, Old Catton, Norwich. For once someone (the vicar) called him Herbert Edward.

Bertie Boulter DFC, Tom Empson DFC, RNZAF, Tommy Broom DFC**, with the Mosquito as the appropriate backdrop at the Pathfinders' fiftieth anniversary, RAF Wyton, August 1992.

Darr Aero Tech control tower, through the rigging of a PT17 Stearman.

Christine and Bertie preparing for take-off.

Bertie and Christine Boulter and No.28.

The Darr Aero Tech fleet – Boeing PT17 Stearman primary trainer stretching almost as far as the eye can see.

The restoration team for No.28: Bertie Boulter, Dave Bagshaw and Jim Avis, posing for the press.

Bertie at home in Saxlingham Nethergate, Norfolk.

could keep up with him. I couldn't blame him, that one was far too close for comfort. We then went on ten days' leave. Jim went off to Tunbridge Wells, I went home to see Mum.

The Ford Eight took Bertie back to Norwich for Christmas celebrations with his mother and aunt and uncle. It was 28 December when he and Jim were back in action. Their names were on the battle order for an operation to Frankfurt. There was a lot of cloud cover that night and they spent half the time they were airborne on instruments. Again it was a single 4,000 pound bomb load that they delivered. Amazingly that trip took Bertie's log-book past 1,100 hours. He had had over 1,025 prior to his first operation; yet here he was nineteen operations later, only adding seventy or so to the total. At the end of October, he and Jim had been the new boys, now as the New Year approached they were old hands at the job.

On 30 December they were assigned an NFT on PF404. It was quite a long process for once with quite a number of systems needing a thorough check before the plane could be passed out as fit for service. Obviously their thoroughness in the test proved justified, as they were allocated 404 the following day for a late-afternoon operation to Berlin. This was to be their fifth raid on the German capital. They landed back at Wyton at 20.50 hours on New Year's Eve after almost five hours in the air and so brought their year to a successful conclusion. Germany was very much in the final stages of its retreat and according to the news of the day the war was definitely now drawing to a close. Those in the know were aware of this, but also aware that its fanatical leaders were still a long way short of surrendering, so the pressure still had to be maintained on the crumbling Nazi regime and there would be no let-up for the bomber crews in 1945. There were New Year's Eve celebrations in the Wyton mess that evening. However they were not extensive as the squadron was scheduled to be on operations the next day.

I had been allocated to share a room with Tommy Broom when I moved from Warboys to Wyton. That turned out to be quite an experience I can tell you. Tommy was the bar officer for several bars at Wyton, and as with all things he did, any mess he was associated with just had to be a success. He made sure of that. This mess activity was the only area where the Flying Brooms were not equal. Tommy enjoyed a pint, or two, or three, Ivor was a non drinker. Simple situations demanded simple solutions: Tommy drank Ivor's beer for him, it was never a problem.

With Tommy's social activities came an occasional display of his antisocial sense of humour. I'm not sure if he personally threw the odd Very cartridge into the mess fire or not, but it was not a totally uncommon occurrence at that time, though getting enough colours up the chimney to alert the station fire brigade only happened once to my knowledge. Also Tommy was not averse to the odd practical joke, including wake-up calls in the middle of the night and a whole variety of well-practised pranks on the unsuspecting. It did mean that there were quite a few chaps all waiting to get their own back on him. Being Tommy's room mate meant I was involved whether I wanted to be or not. I can recall on several occasions having quickly to barricade the door to prevent raiders entering, armed with heaven knows what to disrupt our much-needed sleep – well, my sleep anyway. Tommy's sleeping draft of a pint or two of the local brew often meant he slept through the whole thing however loud or raucous it became.

Amazingly come 07.00 hours the next day he was always up, alert, bright and disgustingly cheerful. I on the other hand, had by then become greatly attached to my bed and often wished to stay there. Any suggestion to the contrary could be met with a fusillade of mutinous grumbles and mutterings. A lathering from his shaving brush, on a regular basis, was his main tool for persuading me that his was in fact the correct line of thought at that time of day, not mine.

To give you some idea how soundly Tommy slept, on one occasion several of the chaps broke into our room one night and undid his pyjama top, unfolded his arms and slapped a huge bacon rind, previously 'liberated' from the mess kitchen, on his chest. They then re-folded his arms over the smelly object and re-buttoned his pyjamas. The noise alone woke me up – Tommy slept through the whole thing. No doubt he later returned the favour in full measure; mess life was like that at Wyton. Life was never dull with Tommy around. Some time later we were subjected to another attack, which must have been executed very quietly, as neither Tommy nor I woke up. This time they managed to cut off one half of Tommy's moustache, and left it in such a state that he had to shave it all off . This caused such concern for Tommy's state of mind that 1409 Met Flight composed and donated to Tommy the following verses, printed with his permission. I remember thinking they were brilliant when I first saw them, and, half a century later, they still bring a smile to my face.

> It burst in bounteous raggedness,
> From whence no man can tell.
> Quite seasonless, a lovely growth
> In winter's icy spell.
>
> Tenderly, with precious care
> Every little bristle grew.
> Each showing from its very birth
> The will to bloom anew.
>
> But from whence its strength? From what deep seat
> Can this fine spirit spring?
> Which, in short weeks, makes Armstrong's look
> A trickle of a thing.

In just a month, he could well whack
All other sorties flown.
A goodly sprint – and he could make
A take off on his own.

Trim it not: but this time, let
Its sweeping grandeur flow,
Its ends uplifted to the stars,
Its centre – toecap low.

Keep it strong and fine and free,
Beyond all human match.
Where birds may nest, and maidens come
To shelter 'neath its thatch.

But lest in endless beer and smoke
The lesser bristles bleach,
Just one last plea . . . ..another pipe
Of slightly longer reach!

I missed him greatly when he got his promotion to squadron
leader, as that entitled him to a room of his own, though I
have to admit it did allow a regular degree of sanity to re-
enter my life in off-duty hours.

CHAPTER EIGHT

January 1945

During the first days of 1945 the raids on Germany continued much the same as they had during the previous year. On 1 January Bertie and Jim were on the battle order for a return trip to Hanover, a city they had raided almost two months earlier. Others, including Ivor and Tommy Broom went off on a daylight raid to attack railway tunnels near Kaiserslautern. As each tunnel went through a hill, the only way to get the bombs into them was through the mouths. It needed a lot of practice and quite a bit of patience from the crews as they got used to the idea of bombing nearly 20 feet off the ground rather than their normal operational altitude of 25,000 feet.

Quite a number of us were selected to train for this, though we all knew from the outset that not all of us would be going. We had several practice sessions during the run-up period, along the edge of the Wash, just out from King's Lynn. There was a marker set up in the mud flats and we had to arrive at low level and literally 'lob' the bombs along the shallows at the marker. It was not easy. In fact at first I even found it difficult to judge the point of release to achieve a near miss. We were using the standard 11 pound practice bombs and usually managed six goes at it before we had to return to Wyton.

For low-level bombing it was the pilot who knew best

when to release the bomb. This was not a new technique, but for those of us unfamiliar with it, it took a fair amount of learning and practice. At first I got too close before pressing the release button; then of course, I had to pull up somewhat smartly to avoid the target. On the next set of attempts I released early and pulled up far too soon. Eventually, after quite a few days' practice, some of the bombs started to fall in their correct place. We were now starting to get somewhere. For the raid, the front-facing camera would capture the tunnel entrance and the rear-facing camera the exit. This involved the shallow approach we had practised over the Wash, flying straight with no slipping or skidding, then opening the throttle immediately after releasing the bomb, followed by a steep climb over the hill, then throttling back and diving down to low level to allow the rear-facing camera to record the results.

Ivor then moved the practice area back to the airfield at Wyton, where the rifle-firing butts became the centre of attention. We all got four or five goes at this and I have to say it was great fun to be officially roaring across the airfield like a hooligan at roof height, particularly when you realized that the flight commander was in the plane immediately in front of you doing the same thing. We did this in all conditions and some crews had seven or eight practice sessions. We did not stop even for bad weather. I can remember standing on the airfield hearing one of the crews doing the low pass towards the butts, but being unable to see the plane due to the mist. It certainly got a bit hairy at times. Despite our practice, or maybe because of it, Jim and I did not get picked for the tunnel raids. I happily returned the bombing responsibility back to Jim. We did however get picked for the Hanover raid.

The operation to Hanover had a late-afternoon start in Mosquito PF 410 with four 500 pounders as ordnance. It took about half an hour longer to get there and back than on the previous visit, but due to the early start they were still back by 21.30 hours. It was rather a long trip and included an hour and a half on instruments. It was only on their return they heard of the success of the Kaiserslautern tunnel raid by the five crews who had taken part in the operation. Ivor and Tommy and scored a bull's eye and were rewarded with a gush of steam and smoke billowing from their tunnel exit.

> We definitely thought that we got the easiest target that day. The boys on the tunnel trip had to work devilish hard to hit their target and then avoid bumping into the surrounding countryside. Ivor earned the second bar to his DFC leading that one, and Tommy got his first bar to his. Sadly the Wellstead/Mullen crew in PF 411 were lost when their Mosquito crashed on take-off due to the failure of one engine. As usual, Tommy's navigation had been spot on and Ivor's flying had matched it. They dropped their single 4,000 pounder straight down the tunnel entrance behind an unsuspecting freight train. It was only later that we found out that this was a signifi-cant materials supply route for the German troops taking part in the offensive now known as the Battle of the Bulge. The German campaign ended twelve days later with the tunnels still out of action. We like to think that the raid helped shorten that particular German offensive, and ultimately the war itself.

A couple of NFTs on the 3rd and 4th led up to Bertie and Jim's sixth trip to Berlin, on the evening of the 4th. That went fine, but the repeat visit on the following evening in PF 415 was quite different and had a number of far-reaching conse-quences. When they got to the aircraft the ground crew were still working on it, and it did not look like a quick tweak here or there; it looked as if a somewhat more substantial engineering operation was being undertaken.

When we were dropped off at dispersal by the aircrew coach we found that all the panels were off the starboard engine and there were a number of the mechanics working on it by torchlight, behind a very inadequate canvas windbreak in the freezing cold. After talking with them, I contacted the squadron commander by phone and explained to him that the chiefy thought it would take more than half an hour to complete what they were doing and have the plane ready for service. From the warmth of his cosy office he told me to wait for the work to be completed and follow the rest of the squadron to Berlin. On take-off, just before becoming airborne, the starboard engine began to emit intermittent flames from the exhausts, accompanied by a simultaneous loss of power. Each time this happened, some really firm corrective rudder and aileron inputs were required to prevent a roll to the right. We were fortunate that it at least continued to run, however badly, and provide some power to help the situation. With our attention firmly fixed on the dying engine we again headed to the jettison area at 5200N 0235E and relieved ourselves of the 4,000 pounder. It would be fair to say neither plane nor crew were very happy on the return trip to the emergency runway at Woodbridge, although we knew we could make it, even if the delinquent engine stopped producing power altogether.

Jim and I had worked together for a while now and it was obvious to me that he was decidedly unhappy. He elaborated on this while we were awaiting transport back to Wyton; so when he suggested we had a cup of tea and a chat the next day, it was no real surprise that he said he wanted to finish operational flying. He explained that after the various mishaps in the past few weeks he just felt that someone was trying to tell us something, and the take-off on more or less one engine was the last straw. Having baled out over France and returned to continue to complete a further twelve or more operations, he was fully entitled to make that decision, and left 128 Squadron with no stain on his character or record. Sadly it did mean, as these things often did in war time, it was to be the last time I ever saw him. He had been a great guy to fly with. At this time Chris Hart's pilot had been posted, but for totally different reasons; thus I inherited him as a navigator, and he got me as his pilot. Again time would prove it was another crew combination that worked extremely well.

Our first operation together was the next day, on the 7th. We were aboard PF 403, a Mk XXV and we were part of a 100-plus raid on Nuremburg. It all went rather well and uneventfully. I then had a week's leave and met up with Chris again on the 14th for an NFT in an old favourite of mine, MM 204. Our next trip together was not as smooth as some and would be the end of the line for MM 204. For some time now Berlin had been attacked on a nightly basis by the Light Night Striking Force [LNSF] – so regularly in fact that some aircrews called it the Milk Run. It was all part of the whirlwind that Bomber Harris had promised the Germans that they would reap. A break in this retribution was considered highly undesirable.

The weather forecast during the day was not good and very high westerly winds were forecast for the evening at our operating height. It was also forecast that the weather over England at low level would deteriorate markedly later in the night and as a result, the heavy bombers would not operate at all as the trip would have simply taken them too long. However the BBC still needed to be able to announce to the British public the next morning, 'Last night our aircraft again bombed Berlin.' The met men considered that there was a reasonable chance that the Mosquitos of the LNSF would be fast enough to get back before the predicted front bearing rain, mist and murk arrived.

Six planes each from six squadrons were subsequently

detailed for Berlin. One crashed on take-off and so thirty-five Mosquitos set off to demoralize further the citizens of the Fatherland. The met men had forecast a 120 knot tail wind at 25,000 feet which we soon found out was grossly understating it. We overshot Berlin, easily beating the marker aircraft to the target area. Before we had started even to realize our situation we saw two searchlights switch on with their beams vertical. Then slowly they descended, converged their beams together, pointing in the reciprocal direction to our track, and were then extinguished. This was repeated a second time. Now we knew for sure they were pointing to Berlin. The only troops in that area likely to do that were Russian. They must have identified us by the engine noise of our Merlin engines, and worked out that we had overshot. We had hardly completed half of our 180 degree turn to sort ourselves out when we saw the PFF markers in the distance. It seemed to take a long time to return and to reposition ourselves to make a successful bombing run, but eventually we did and then turned again for home, still battling the fierce upper winds that had fooled us in the first place.

Eventually, well over three hours' flying time later we identified Woodbridge beneath us, with the glow from the lights of their massive runway showing through a layer of cloud. We were given the cloud base of 1,100 feet and Chris estimated Wyton in twelve minutes. What a surprise it was to us when we descended in to Wyton that the weather had closed in dramatically. We could see nothing as we drew close, flying the standard beam approach for a straight-in landing. At circuit height we could still not see the lights. On final, dead on the beam, we could still see absolutely nothing. Final approach – nothing; passing the outer marker at 600 feet – still nothing; 150 feet and down to zero at the set QFE (Atmospheric Pressure at Aerodrome Elevation) on the altimeter and still not a glimmer. We instigated overshoot procedures and went round again. Whilst on this circuit we heard F/O Allan Heitman DFC, RAAF and his navigator P/O Gould make their last call; they announced they were out of fuel and both engines had stopped. They didn't make it.

Our second and third attempts to land were equally unsuccessful. I told Chris we would not be making another approach, we had run our main tanks virtually dry until the engines spluttered and now the inners must have been almost empty. No sooner had I finished saying that, and before Chris could answer, than the voice of Ivor Broom came through loud and clear on the R/T. 'Bertie. This is Ivor Broom. This is not a request, this is an order. Climb immediately to a safe height and bale out . . . Acknowledge.' I acknowledged. At 5,000 feet I levelled out and Chris and I abandoned MM 204 to her fate.

Once again a muddy field awaited me after my second try at parachuting. It was getting to be a bad habit. Maybe Jim had been right, maybe he had a point. With the wet fog clinging like a scotch mist, I wandered along the hedgerow until I found an opening onto a narrow road and turned left to see where it got me. The time would have been about 02.30. Shortly after this I came to a farm-house by the side of the road. I recall it was on my left. I walked up to the door and knocked hard. After a while the first-floor window above me opened and a voice from above my head asked what I wanted. I explained that I was an RAF pilot and had baled out of my Mosquito returning from a raid on Berlin and asked if I could please use their telephone. The voice hardened and advised me there was a public phone box 200 yards down the road on the right-hand side. The window then slammed shut. Somewhat stunned at this sort of response I continued my wandering down the lane, thinking mainly how I was going to get through to Wyton. I had no money on me, due to my usual pre-operation procedures and added to that was the fact that I hadn't really got a clue who to call anyway. Even when I had decided on that, would the operator put me through to an operational RAF station at that time of the morning? As these things buzzed through my mind, I became aware of the sound of engines, the rumble of vehicle tyres and a dull glow of some masked headlights coming up behind me. I looked round. Amazingly it was an American staff car, followed by a large truck with some mini-searchlights on it, scouring the hedges on the side of the lane. Bringing up the rear was an ambulance, into which I was quickly bundled.

It appeared that a rather alert sentry at the nearby USAAF airfield of Thurleigh (later to become RAE Bedford) had heard the crash of MM 204 and had alerted the chaps who now had me in their charge. As all this was at a very unsociable time of the day, I was mightily impressed. The first port of call at Thurleigh was the sick quarters where I was thoroughly checked out and had some attention to the front of my shins. Once again on baling out, I had managed to skin them. I mentally made a note to avoid exiting any further Mossies in flight, or at least to devise for myself a less painful method of getting through that hatch. Naturally I was somewhat vociferous about my reception by the local farmer and my native Canadian accent became more pronounced the more excited I got, even after several years in the RAF, with the last one as an officer!

The American MO tried valiantly to make me feel better by telling me that the farmer must have mistaken me for a drunken USAAF airman – it really didn't have the affect that he had hoped. Meanwhile the rescue crew had set off again in the unfavourable conditions to see if they could locate Chris. They came back an hour or so later without finding him. The next morning we found out why. Chris had worked out that being found was quite a long shot in the middle of the night. Normally he slept at night, therefore he would go to sleep now. He had vast quantities of protective parachute material to wrap around himself, which he proceeded to do, then promptly fell asleep until it became daylight. He was still asleep when a passing farm hand found him on his way to work. I really had to think more about this baling out business. Both my trusty colleagues had got it far better sorted than I had. Jim met up with some decent coves and got well drunk, and Chris realized that he might as well get some sleep, whilst both times I spent several hours each night wandering around, lost in the mist and rain with very sore shins. Someone was doing it right, and it wasn't me. Later that morning the C of E padre from Wyton drove over to Thurleigh Aerodrome to collect me. We picked Chris up on the way back to the airfield.

Ivor and Tommy Broom had been on the same raid, and had managed to find Berlin first time. Because of this they were back at Wyton about twenty minutes ahead of the returning squadron. The weather had already deteriorated to a near impossible situation when the flying Brooms arrived back. They had visibility problems on approach too, but just as Ivor initiated the overshoot, Tommy caught a fleeting glimpse of the runway lights. He was then able to instruct Ivor on the heading and timed him round the circuit for a procedural approach. They landed successfully and were in fact the last plane to land at Wyton that night. By now, as they taxied in, Ivor was fuming. He taxied directly to the control tower, shut down, leaped out of the aircraft and bounded up the stairs. There he ordered the lights to be changed to runway 26, the longest on the airfield and the one served with the standard beam approach. He then verbally ejected the 'regular' squadron CO from the tower and called all 128 Squadron aircraft still airborne to bale out.

Of the thirty-six planes sent on that operation twelve were lost, all of them over East Anglia when they were almost home. Shortly after this the CO was posted. W/Cdr Ernest Rodley took over in his place. He was a real 'flying' CO, and knew how to run an operational squadron.

CHAPTER NINE

February 1945

Unbeknown to Bertie and Chris, or anyone else on 128 Squadron for that matter, late in January, Ivor had been called in to see AVM Don Bennett at his HQ at Castle Hill House, RAF Huntingdon (now home to the local council offices), just a mile or so off the main A1 trunk road. The conversation had been typically short and sweet: 'Ivor, you are promoted to acting wing commander . . . We are having a new squadron at Wyton . . . You are in charge . . . You start forming it tomorrow morning and will be operational by tomorrow evening . . . It will be 163 Squadron . . . Any questions? No, . . . thought not. Well done, off you go. Good luck.'

That's how Ivor and Tommy became 163 Squadron's first crew. Chris and I followed a week later as crew ten or eleven. We joined as the planes became available. The squadron was located across the airfield from 128 Squadron in the very large ex-Lancaster hangar on the south side of the site. True to his word the previous week, AVM Don Bennett had also provided Ivor with a nucleus of his ground crew. In fact 250 men of assorted trades all turned up later that morning. Sadly they had all been working on Wellingtons up until the day before. Not one of them had ever laid a finger, never mind a spanner, on a Mosquito. However they were a pretty good bunch of chaps and soon got the hang of their new charges. Later that day six Mossies of differing ages flew in. They were all Mk XXVs with the Packard-built Merlins, as opposed to the XVIs of 128 Squadron which had the Rolls Royce-built Merlins. They had all been scrounged from a variety of unsuspecting and I expect rather unwilling donor squadrons. Fortunately the Mossies arrived at the onset of some bad weather. This gave Ivor and Tommy (now promoted to squadron leader and squadron navigation officer) a very short breathing space to start to get themselves organized. It was a beginning. 'Small acorns and all that,' as one wag remarked at the bar during those first few, non-flying, days. Little did they know.

By 1 February, the weather had cleared and all six planes were fully serviceable. The new crew chiefs were confident enough to release them to the pilots and Ivor was not about to disappoint the waiting German defences any longer. As part of his scheme of playing 'catch-up', some planes went twice that day. The first wave of all six planes went to Berlin and Hamborn, then at 20.00 hours that same evening three planes, KB 510, KB 474 and KB 511 were refuelled, double-checked and sent back to Berlin with fresh crews. According to squadron records, it was noted that this was the first time this type of double operation had ever been mounted. All planes returned safely from both operations. Meanwhile Bertie and Chris cooled their heels at 128 Squadron for a few days, awaiting the arrival of the additional planes.

In the first few days of 163 being operational, Ivor was assigned a squadron adjutant who knew King's Regulations through and through. To Ivor, who had never so much as set foot inside the lecture room of an officers' training establishment, never mind read the manuals, this transfer of 'Dizzie' Davies from 1655 MTU was a real godsend. A lot of the crews knew him already from their training days, and what is more he was an officer able to adapt easily to Ivor's slightly unconventional method of command and assist in the running of the squadron accordingly. Ivor's method was based on two fundamentals learned from two of his previous COs, Hugh Pughe Lloyd, (while based on Malta) and Don Bennett. One was that men of inferior rank were not inferior men and the other that a good commander leads by commanding respect not by demanding respect. Whether on the ground or in the air Ivor always led from the front and Bertie, Chris and the other crews of 163 would follow him to a man.

Chris and I had an easy start in February. I did a couple of NFTs when I came back off leave, one with Sgt Severson on the 7th and one with Chris on 8th, the morning of our second trip to Berlin together. It was a latish start, and we were last away of the five planes to go that night. The weather had been pretty average all day, with intermittent light rain, though it cleared sufficiently once we left the coast to enable us to head to our target. I logged just an hour on instruments that flight. Our take-off time had been 21.10 hours, and our touchdown time just over four hours later at 01.12 hours. It was the quickest we had made it to the German capital and back so far, for the whole of the war. In fact it was a speed that we were never able to match again. The next day we were not on operations and a solitary fifty-minute NFT was our only duty of the day. After we landed the weather started to clamp down and the operations were cancelled for the night anyway. No one was particularly surprised.

Once the front had moved through overnight, the skies over Wyton cleared and we took KB 510 on an NFT in preparation for a raid on Hanover. This would make it my fifth visit there. This time it was with four 500 pounders as cargo. We were number two for take-off behind Ivor and Tommy, and we were third to land, again only a few minutes behind them. I felt good about that until I learned F/Lt Colby and Sgt Richard in KB 526 had managed to take off five minutes behind us, and still get home immediately in front of Ivor and Tommy; that was darned good going. I remember thinking that despite that they would still be behind Tommy in the bar whatever happened; that was always going to be inevitable. We all had encountered quite a lot of searchlights, but little effective flack, apart from F/O Martin who must have strayed a little off course on his way in and upset a German ack-ack battery somewhere along the way. It happened like that some nights.

The weather clamped back down on the 11th with a mixture of rain and sleet blowing about. Very little moved on the airfield that day and to be honest I don't remember seeing too much constructive activity at all. However, two days after the raid on Hanover we were off to Stuttgart. The weather was still less than hopeful in the morning, but it eased off a bit after lunch, and by take-off time in the late afternoon it was at least flyable. It cleared soon after take-off and was OK all the way through to the target, though I remember there was some cloud over Stuttgart when we flew the bombing run. The bombing seemed on target to us, and we saw two really large explosions in the target area. Fortunately for us there was no flack, which probably indicated that the night fighters were about. Luckily we didn't see any of them either. We landed just after 21.30 hours after a little over three and a half hours in the air.

We were picked for operations again the following day. Our target was Bohlen; three other crews came with us, two went to Bonn and four to Magdeburg. We got home just after midnight, but the crews who went to Bonn had a late start and were not back home until after 02.00 hours. Ivor and F/O Price were detailed on the Magdeburg raid. Each of them saw one of the new Messerschmitt Me 262 jet fighters, and there was no certainty it was even the same one. That was a bit worrying. Our speed supremacy would easily be overcome by the jets if what we had been told was true.

Fortunately on the night the 262 did not take an interest in either of the Mosquitos from 163 Squadron.

The squadron stood down the following day; then just to add a further contribution to the war, the weather clamped down in the Huntingdon area for the next four days and all operations were cancelled due to very poor visibility. It was not until the 19th that the station was able to resume operations, and even then it was doubtful until after lunch that day whether the visibility would clear sufficiently to allow this to happen. In the meantime Bertie followed tradition and spent almost an hour and a half in the Link Trainer keeping his hand in and practising. It was well known that the squadron commander did his share in the Link and there was therefore no excuse for any other pilots to duck out. Having managed an NFT on the 18th, Bertie and Chris were not particularly surprised to be picked for the six-plane raid on Erfurt on the 19th. Little did they know that they would fly every day now until the beginning of March, and then sometimes twice or even three times a day. They were going to be remarkably busy.

For the Erfurt raid, Bertie and Chris, reunited with KB 403 again, were the third plane in the air at 17.57 hours; at 17.57 plus thirty seconds, KB 511 crewed by F/O Price and Sgt O'Shea were also airborne. That was as close as anyone needed to be on a night take-off, though they did try to use alternate sides of the runway in a stream take-off. On landing later that evening two other Mosquitos, KB 505 and KB 615, managed to touch down within a minute of each other; close again. Considering it was after a four-hour round trip, including at least an hour of instrument flying, that was astonishingly close timing. It had been a relatively easy night with all crews reporting no opposition and evidence of fires and explosions in the target area. Again the next night, on the runs to Berlin and Mannheim, there was only a small amount of flak reported by the crews who went to Berlin and none at all from the three planes that went to Mannheim. Bertie and

Chris spent an hour and a half on instruments, but still made it home by 22.30 hours after being airborne for four and a quarter hours.

All in all, things were getting easier. The opposition was getting less, that was both flak and fighters, as well as searchlights. We were getting used to what we were doing and of course the Mk XXV with the lighter bomb load was a much easier plane to fly than the Mk XVI carrying a 4,000 pounder as there was less tendency to swing on take-off. I remember Ivor admitting that on at least one occasion the swing had even got the better of him and he had to slow the plane with a lot of right brake, turn it on the grass and backtrack for a second go.

It may have been getting easier, but it was pretty busy. I recall that it all seemed to merge into a continuous operation with sleep and food thrown at us at fairly regular but unpredictable intervals. Still it was the same for everyone, and being young it never seemed to bother us. We went back to Berlin on the 22nd, and to Worms on the 23rd, before returning to Berlin on the 26th and 27th. I remember the last operation of the month was a real pain as we did not set off until nearly 01.00 hours. Needless to say it was almost daylight by the time we got back to Wyton. The squadron stood down on the 28th and we all slept in and had a good rest – boy did we need it. Perversely the weather was pretty good that day, probably better than anything that we had had for most of the operations during the previous few weeks; What we didn't know then was that the first day of March was also going to be busy.

Amazingly when Bertie presented his log book for Ivor to sign off his February summary, he still had only 1,217 hours. Operational bomber flying had added less than 175 hours to the total since his first raid on Germany five months ago.

CHAPTER TEN

March 1945

O n 1 March, in generally improving weather, Ivor and Bertie took Oxford AB 754 from Wyton to Horsham St Faith (now known as Norwich International Airport). It was the first time they had flown together in anything, and was a round trip of just one hour. The Airspeed Oxford AB 754 was the station hack, a sort of equivalent of today's works' truck or pool car. Bertie also had the NFT to do in KB 403 that day, then of course there was a return trip to Berlin once again; it was his thirteenth operation to that battered city. By now the Allied ground troops were getting ever closer and the Russian army was virtually banging on the city gates.

I decided not to tell Chris that it was to be my thirteenth visit to Berlin. It seemed better to keep that sort of thing to myself. We were the last of the ten planes to take off that night, and lifted off Wyton's runway at exactly 18.30 hrs. We logged five hours for the trip, but during the debrief the eagle-eyed intelligence officer noted it as five hours and one minute for the Boulter/Hart crew in the squadron records. I was never quite sure how they worked that out or why they did it like that. I guessed it was something to do with being keen on admin and paperwork, but I was never really sure. One or two of the crews took some twenty minutes longer for the same journey. It was not an unusual time spread across the squadron for a similar trip, despite following the same route at the same height in similar aircraft, particularly remembering we all got to the target area within a minute or so of each other. One trip by the squadron to Worms in the previous month had a spread of nearly fifty minutes across the airborne times of all the planes and one to Berlin later in the month would easily match it. I'm sure we were not unique and it was the same on other squadrons. It was never discussed unless one of the crews had encountered a real problem of some sort, and to be honest even things like engine failures were often met with comments like, 'Yes, we had that happen last trip.' We all knew the ground crews would sort it before the next trip, or we would be allocated another plane.

By now the squadron strength was building and new crews were joining on a regular basis. The first week of March saw six new crews arrive within five days, with more to follow; though on 5 March F/Lt Colby left to take over as 'A' Flight commander on 571 Squadron, just down the road at RAF Oakington. Now with the squadron getting nearer to full strength, 163 were often able to commit ten or twelve planes to an operation on a nightly basis. The ground crews were fantastic, and because of this the squadron was able to follow this pattern for the next two weeks without a break. It was a really tremendous effort from both aircrew and ground crew alike.

Chris and I drew no duties at all on the 2nd; we were perhaps seeing the benefit of a few more crews about the place. We were, however, on the list for the raid to Berlin on the 3rd. Once again we were in our favourite plane, KB 403. The NFT included some standard beam approach practice and took over an hour. We did make up for this lengthy NFT by completing the raid on Berlin and back in four hours and ten minutes, our second fastest run to the German capital ever, though we did notice that the markers seemed a bit scattered that night, as was the subsequent bombing pattern. We took comfort from the fact that in a city like Berlin any bomb dropped had to cause damage.

We had a change of plane and target for the 6th. Chris and I were allocated KB 541 for the Essen raid. Again it was one of those very early morning starts that I disliked and we were last away at just after 02.00 hrs. We had a good run both there and back and I cannot recall seeing either fighters or flak; I noticed in the debrief notes, neither did any of the rest of the crews. There was a separate operation to Berlin the same night, and the four crews from 163 all had a similar opposition-free operation, although P/O Reg Topley got caught out by getting into someone else's slipstream, which caused his plane to invert and lose 10,000 feet before he could sort himself out and get it all back under control again. Not a nice experience.

We had the next day off, then got selected for a daylight raid on Wesel, just over the Dutch border on the northern edge of the Ruhr industrial area. It was quite strange to be taking off in daylight and even stranger to be heading out across the North Sea with full, clear visibility. There were six planes that took off from Wyton and we joined up with forty or so others to complete the formation. There was quite a bit of cloud cover as we headed over the water towards mainland Europe and by the time we got to the target area it was 10/10ths cover, we could see nothing on the ground. We were totally relying on the OBOE (Blind Bombing System) leader to mark the aiming point with the usual accuracy. Our line-astern stepped formation was easy to fly; but for some reason the formation leader slowed more than was planned and we were forced to throttle back and raise the aircraft nose to keep station. Unlike the Americans, we bombed the targets individually, and not just when we saw the target indicators released, so each navigator still operated in the usual way. Under the circumstances it was all a bit frustrating; however we all made it back. It took just three hours fifteen to complete the raid.

The raid on Munster the next day was back to normal. Three of the 163 Mosquitos were on a 'spoof' raid to confuse the German command. It must have worked as they later found that there were simultaneous raids on Munster, Berlin, Dessau, Harburg and the oil refinery at Heide that night. The last three targets shared in excess of 1,000 heavy bombers between them. When Bertie and Chris got to their target there was partial cloud cover, but visibility was sufficient for a successful bombing run. The marker flares were dropped and immediately prompted half a dozen searchlights to become active, which in turn stirred up a nearby heavy flak battery. Both Bertie and F/Lt Bowen reported flying through a stream of heavy bombers on the outward journey, though which raid the heavies were on was, of course, not known; there was a lot going on that night. The crews allocated to the Berlin raid also reported an easy run with just a small amount of light flak. All the aircraft from 163 Squadron got home from their 'daylight' sorties, though the port engine of KB 510 kept cutting out on its anxious crew throughout the operation. Bertie and Chris were then due some leave, and the problems started.

About this time Chris had got into a spot of bother. He got sent to the RAF correction centre in Sheffield for two weeks, lost six months' seniority, acquired a gorgeous wife and was awarded the DFM, all within the space of a few weeks. It would probably make sense actually to recount the story in some semblance of order to make it understandable. Chris was friendly with a WAAF corporal in sick quarters and the friendship was now at the serious stage. He knew a young New Zealand navigator who offered to sell him a spare RAF navigator's watch he had somehow managed to acquire. The deal was done and Chris duly presented the watch to his young lady. Shortly after, the young New Zealander was killed on a raid over Germany and almost simultaneously the young WAAF's senior officer noticed the non-standard timepiece that she was using. Questions were asked and Chris was made aware that he was in a spot of bother. Unsurprisingly he was not his usual self and his concentration and confidence took a bit of a knock. He also got sick a couple of times over the target, which was very unlike him.

It was about this time Ivor suggested one lunchtime that we might like a three-day leave pass. I phoned Chris in the sergeants mess only to be advised that he didn't really want any leave as he had recently had a falling out with his father and didn't want to go home to Derby at the moment. I didn't mind, so I popped along and told Ivor. 'OK, it's your choice, but you have earned it you know,' was his answer.

A short time later, still during lunchtime, Chris phoned back. 'Bertie, I've changed my mind. I've asked my girl to marry me. I want to go on leave and get married.'

I went back to Ivor. He was totally unflustered. 'OK, it's your choice Bertie. Enjoy your leave.'

Three days later I got back; six days later Chris and his new wife returned. Now he had been AWOL for three days which compounded the problem with the watch. At the court of enquiry, Chris's new wife could not testify against him, so she was not present, and as the young New Zealand navigator was not around to defend himself Chris elected to say nothing. Two weeks in the Sheffield Aircrew Correction Centre and a six-month lack of seniority were handed down (He was just about to be made flight sergeant before all this cropped up). I therefore spent the next weeks flying with a variety of navigators.

In the meantime I learned that F/Lt Cooper and F/Sgt Gillespie were still missing from a raid on Berlin, and that KB 476 had encountered an engine problem and crash landed in Holland with F/O Harris and F/O Wynes aboard, although both Harris and Wynes were already back and on flying duties again. F/O Drake was my navigator on an NFT on my regular KB 403 and F/O Howell then took over to come with me on the raid on Bremen. We had three 500 pounders and cluster flares in the bomb bay as we thundered down Wyton's familiar runway at just after 02.30 hrs on a rather cold spring morning. We actually overshot the target and had to orbit to complete our bomb run, but despite that we had a pretty uneventful flight and landed back at 05.55, debriefed and headed off for a well-earned breakfast. I somehow guessed we would be on operations the following evening, I was not wrong.

After what seemed the briefest of time in bed we were up and preparing for yet another raid on Berlin. It was an almost perfect spring day, with a forecast of continuing good weather. W/O Boyle had drawn the short straw and would be coming with me in KB 555, a plane that I had not flown for over a month, almost since the start of the affair between KB 403, Chris and myself. We were dispatched that evening in two waves, the first wave of 106 Mosquitos heading off at about 19.00 hrs and our second wave of a further thirty-six planes following just before 02.00 hrs. KB 425 did not make it. It returned early with engine trouble and crash landed at Upwood. Both crew members survived the crash but sadly died of their injuries later in Ely hospital. The navigator was F/O Drake who had flown the NFT with me just the previous day. The news came through from Upwood before the first wave got back. It seemed ironic and unfair that he had died and I had just been awarded my DFC; but then war was never meant to be fair.

The four hours twenty-five I logged for that Berlin trip was to be my last operation for March. However there were still a few NFTs to be flown to keep my hand in.

Chris was back in circulation about this time, but Ivor had a further surprise for him. When he reported in to the squadron adjutant's office, Ivor heard him arrive and suggested he come in to have a chat. After the recently revitalized salute, Ivor told Chris to stand easy. I had told Ivor that Chris and his dad were not on the best of terms and obviously this was not Ivor's view of how things should be. He suggested that Chris take a further three day pass and go to Derby, make his peace with his dad and take his new bride with him. Ivor would see that the new Mrs Hart had all the appropriate leave documents sorted by later that afternoon. When he hesitated, Ivor reminded him that it was still a suggestion at the moment, though it could of course soon become an order. The suggestion was accepted.

Chris told me later that his dad was waiting for him when he arrived, and the ensuing conversation went more or less like this.

'Well done son, congratulations.'

'Thanks dad, she is quite something isn't she?'

'She is indeed, but I actually meant your DFM.'

'My what?'

'Your DFM. Your squadron commander was in touch a few days ago and told me about it. Well done. He told me you got the DFM and your pilot got the DFC. He said he'd leave me to tell you. Though he must have told the local paper, it was in yesterday's edition.'

For once Chris admitted that he was totally lost for words. And that was how Chris, just a few days out of prison, learned of his well-deserved medal. That was Ivor's way of doing things, though those of us who thought that we knew our squadron officers, could smell the involvement of Dizzy and Tommy in the subterfuge from a mile away. Chris's promotion to flight sergeant was promulgated about two weeks later.

While this was going on I did a couple of trips in the station hack, an Oxford AB 754; one to Exeter with Sgt

Killick on the 24th and another to York on the 31st. The one to Exeter was really meant to have been to Culdrose, to attend the funeral of F/O Drake, whose family lived in Falmouth. We never made it. We had left the day before the funeral, but low cloud and poor visibility gripped the West Country and deteoriated the further south and west we went. By the time we gave up and turned back for Exeter we were half a mile out to sea flying along the coast below the level of the cliff tops and the cloud was down to cliff-top height. It was really getting hairy and quite dangerous. We landed at Exeter and took the slow overnight train to Truro. It was a tortuous journey that seemed endless. We got to the family home at 10.30 a.m., just as they returned from church. It had been a very early funeral and we had missed it by an hour. We were desperately sorry and said so to the family. F/O Drake's family were very brave and kind to us as they fed and watered us before we headed back to Exeter to fly home. Needless to say, the worst of the weather had cleared as we took off and headed back to Wyton.

Chris returned to operations on the 28th and we took KB 403 on an NFT for W/O Coxall and W/O Boyle to use on the upcoming raid on Berlin. I suspect we felt that by now 403, along with most of the other Mossies on squadron, could make its own way there without our assistance, they had done that trip so many times.

It would be unrealistic to suggest that despite all their success, all the operations flown by 163 went without a hitch that month. Apart from the two fatalities, there were other incidents that kept everyone on their toes and reminded them that what they were doing was still highly dangerous. It also reminded them that although mortally wounded, Hitler's Third Reich was still a lethal target and more than capable of biting back. Crews were now regularly reporting the sighting of the new Messerschmitt 262 jet fighter, though it was fortunate that they were only sightings not actual head-to-head encounters. To add to that, the planes themselves and the equipment in them sometimes failed and put their crews in very dangerous situations. Apart from the crashes, engine failure affected both KB 510 and KB 502 on the 7th and 8th, then on the 11th and 12th three different crews all experienced severe oxygen problems. On top of that five or six crews encountered all manner of cockpit equipment problems, including the Irwin/Thompson crew having the bombing release button fall apart in F/O Thompson's hand! Needless to say he was not amused to have this happen as he started the bomb run. All the Mosquito crews reluctantly accepted that occasionally they would not drop their bombs as accurately as they wished, for a variety of reasons, but to get all the way to the target and then have to bring the bomb load back because of a relative minor mechanical failure was a bit hard for them to accept.

The Germans were of course not averse to creating problems for the crews, not just with anti-aircraft guns and fighter planes, but also by creating dummy targets using diversionary fires and lights. They were also rumoured to have a trick of firing pyrotechnics, nicknamed scarecrows, prepared to explode in a way that made it look as if two British planes had collided and exploded, though later post-war intelligence throws doubt on this theory. Hamish Mahaddie in particular was sceptical of their existence.

CHAPTER ELEVEN

April 1945

Having only lost one day's flying to weather conditions in March, it came as quite a surprise to the squadron to lose four of the first eight days of the following month to the traditional English April weather, and to have pretty windy conditions for most of the rest of the time. It was, however, able to mount raids up to the 5th of the month and to start again on the 9th. On that day the Mosquitos were made ready for a 22.00 hrs take-off. They were to join a larger group, making a total of fifty-four aircraft. One from another squadron went missing, but the remaining fifty-three got through and hit their primary target.

It was Berlin again. I counted in my log-book that it would be my sixteenth bombing operation on the German capital. Somehow I began to get the feeling that it would soon be the last. Rumours, whether based on fact or fiction, were flying about the camp and of course fuelled by the newspapers, all claiming victory was in sight. The opposition was becoming less and less and more often than not I was telling the intelligence officer in the debriefing room that I had seen neither fighters nor flak. I know the other chaps were all saying much the same. This last trip to Berlin followed that pattern. Only F/Lt Hawley and F/O Richardson saw anything for the whole journey and that was a single burst of tracers that went over their wings. I was teamed up with F/O

Howell again for this one, and it would be the second of three operations we would fly together. We were last away with a take-off time for KB 403 at 22.17 hrs. One or two crews encountered a few searchlights on the way but we didn't. We all seemed to think we had bombed pretty accurately that night and were rather pleased with ourselves. Two huge explosions in the target area were noted at 00.18 hrs, and 00.22 hrs; certainly they both appeared to be much bigger than a single or even a multiple bomb burst. We must have hit something pretty effectively.

F/Lt Jinks and F/Lt Ross managed to bring KB 518 back with some tail damage, but they had no idea how it happened. Like most of the crews, they heard and saw no opposition the whole way there and back; a most odd situation therefore to come back damaged. It was, however, fully repaired and back on line within forty-eight hours, so it could not have been that serious; though as I mentioned earlier, we had a super ground crew who were not known for letting anything get the better of them.

Despite the lousy weather I got in a few NFTs over the next few days and managed to keep my eye in. In fact I managed five over the next seven days including a twenty-minute one on the 10th with F/O Howell in readiness for the raid on Chemnitz. For once we had a really diverse load to deliver; one 500 pounder, one TI [target indicator] and two flares; a real mixed bag in anyone's book. For the first time in a while the weather was pretty much OK all day. It started off overcast and grey, but improved steadily up to take-off time. We were the last crew away of the six heading to Chemnitz, though the squadron log shows we were all airborne within three minutes; KB 623 and KB 555 managing to record identical take-off times, with KB 464 just half a minute ahead of them and KB 508 a further thirty seconds behind. That was a rather busy bit of runway for a short while. We had managed to establish a seventeen-minute spread on our return, which was a bit more like it; I always did like to have the runway to myself. There was a little haze over the target area when we got there, but nothing to speak of. The markers were very scattered and we bombed somewhere close to the centre of them, but I'm not convinced that we had a particularly successful raid, even though it took us nearly five hours to complete it. The crews who went to Berlin had a more adventurous evening and probably a bit more success. One plane was seen to be going down in flames. As KB 502 failed to return with F/O Houghton and F/Sgt Stegman aboard, we had, reluctantly, to assume it had been them. One of the new Me 262 jets was seen again as well as a conventional twin-engined German fighter. Probably it was one of those that got KB 502 as they were on their bombing run, flying straight and level. They would have certainly been at their most vulnerable at that point. The Berlin crews also encountered a fair amount of searchlight activity that night and some moderate flak.

Chris was back with me on the 12th when 163 Squadron went back to Berlin again. The weather was fine and getting warmer, though there were a few thunder showers forming in the afternoon, but they came to little by take-off time, which was just before 22.00 hrs. We had a straightforward run there and back, and encountered very little German activity, except for a large scattering of searchlights close to Berlin. They didn't cone us and chatting to the other pilots after we landed, Bill Jinx was the only one who got coned and then for only two or three minutes before he shook them off. We were back on the conventional four 500 pounders for this one, and they would remain our designated ordnance for the remainder of the war – which only had three more weeks to run, though no-one knew that at the time.

It was on one of these raids to Berlin, either with Chris or one of his replacements whilst he was otherwise engaged in Sheffield, that I had a strange experience that gave me a lot to think about. There was a full moon that particular night and it was almost like daylight at 25,000 feet. There was broken strato-cumulus cloud at 6,000–8,000 feet at about 6/10ths cover. There was no flak as it was a perfect night for the German night fighters. The marker TIs were burning on the ground and easily visible for a good bombing run. I had my head down in the cockpit concentrating on the instruments and we were on to our run-in to the TIs for bombing; everything – heading, height and airspeed – was right. My navigator had been through the 'right . . . left, left' bits and was now saying 'steady, steady' immediately before releasing our four 500 pounders. Despite my concentration I thought I saw a flicker of a shadow out of the corner of my eye, and was compelled to look up to my left. There, within 5 feet of our port wingtip was the fuselage of a Mosquito. Our port propeller was about to chew chunks out of the trailing edge of its starboard wing. I got somewhat excited and told my navigator to 'hold everything' and simultaneously banked to the right in a climbing turn. The other pilot, with his head down, must have seen the shadow of my wingtip over his canopy as he too turned and climbed to his left. I never wanted to get that close to disaster again. Debriefing did not reveal any other aircraft from 128 or 163 squadrons having such a near miss. I could have found out which other squadron may have reported this incident, but at the time it was just one of those things, and knowing who the other crew were wasn't going to achieve anything. I was concentrating hard and the bombs were about to be released; what compelled me to look left? Do we all have some sort of sixth sense, or some sense of close proximity? And why were we so lucky that night?

The Boulter/Hart crew then did an NFT on KB 395 on the 15th and again on the 16th prior to yet another run to Berlin in their favourite plane, KB 403. There were nine aircraft from the squadron on this operation, though for some technical reason, F/O Harris and F/O Wynes in KB 518 were almost a quarter of an hour behind the rest of the planes on take-off. There is no record of them encountering any problems and they completed the raid successfully. One plane was seen going down in flames near the Dutch coast, but all 163's aircraft made it home. The raid was deemed a success as most crews witnessed good bombing concentrations and a lot of smoke and fires in the target area. They also noticed that the Russians were being a real nuisance to the defending Germans and many fires were burning fiercely along their wide, advancing front. F/Lt Hawley and F/O Richardson frightened themselves by getting too close to another unidentified Mosquito and some pretty fancy evasive control input was needed by F/Lt Hawley to avoid an embarrassing crash. Bertie and Chris encountered the odd burst of flak here and there, but were complimentary on debrief about the accuracy of the TIs that night.

By way of a change, we left Berlin alone on the 19th and headed for the airfield at Schleissheim just a few miles north of Munich. It was the beginning of thirty-six hours of repeated bombardment for that particular airfield. We went in the first wave of seven aircraft during the early hours of the morning. We transited out at low level and got our tail assembly peppered for our trouble. It appeared that someone managed a very low trajectory with an AA gun and the shell must have burst just behind us. They got the lot, fin, rudder and ailerons. I don't recall it happening, but someone got lucky as we roared overhead. It was almost certainly down to the Americans, who were in control of that part of liberated France. We had been lucky. A double raid followed the next day with some thirty-six aircraft involved in the second operation and then just to round it off a further four went back that same evening, all with pretty satisfactory results. Again there were several sightings of the new Messerschmitt Me 262 jet fighters by some of the crews, but the jets did not seem that interested in getting involved. Chris and I had not seen one yet; perhaps we were not looking hard enough.

We were on the list again for the operation to Berlin on the 20th. Little did we know it would be our last raid on that battered city and our last operation in dear old KB 403. We did the NFT that afternoon in some decent weather, but with the real threat of thunderstorms approaching according to the met men. We took off just before 22.00 hrs and got back a little after 02.00 hrs. There was a bit more flak about in the target area this time, mainly as we turned after the bomb run and headed for home. It seemed to explode either behind us or way above us and fortunately for us none was anything like close. We thought maybe it was one of the sites we heard that had been manned by schoolchildren and they were less accurate than the experienced adult crews. I guess we'll never know. We did see some explosions on the ground near the target though, so I suspect we were successful again. It was on this trip that Chris and I did actually get to see our first Me 262 jet fighter, at long last. Everyone else on the squadron seemed to have seen at least one or more, long before we did. Chris and I were getting to feel that even the ground crew back at Wyton would get to see them before we did.

During an earlier raid on Kiel on the 21st we lost F/Lt Baker and his navigator F/O Hawthorne. We learned of this on the morning of the 22nd when we went to the squadron office to draw our duties. We knew the war was coming to a close and it seemed particularly harsh with the end so obviously close and the opposition rather thin and ineffective. (We learned a couple of weeks later that F/Lt Baker had survived by parachuting from the remains of KB 529 via the top hatch after a direct hit on the nose. The explosion tore most of the front of the aircraft apart as they were preparing for the bomb run and the bulk of the nose section was totally blown away. F/O Hawthorne, who was by then in his aiming position, stood no chance.)

Operations were cancelled due to dull and very overcast weather conditions that persisted throughout the day on the 22nd. We did a couple more NFTs around Wyton in the murk and gloom that day and again in the clear but frosty conditions that followed on the 23rd; they lasted twenty minutes each. I also managed just over an hour and a half in the Link in two sessions on the 21st and 24th, practising some instrument-flying techniques. In the meantime the squadron sent fourteen aircraft on a raid on the flying-boat pens and anchorages at Travemunde on the Baltic coast of northern Germany. Chris and I missed out on that one. There were rumours that some of the Nazi hierarchy were going to attempt to flee from Europe from there and it seemed a pretty good idea to drop a few bombs to try to stop them. We had sent five planes on a quick 'look-see' sort of raid on the 20th. The operation two days later was the main event and it seemed to be pretty successful.

Three days later another twelve planes from 163 Squadron attacked a second sea-plane pen in the same coastal district at Groszenbrode, with apparently equally successful results. The sea planes were seen and there were several explosions and fires reported as the Mosquitos left the target area. By then I had already headed off to Norwich for a week's leave. Even at home all the talk and all the newspaper headlines were about the war coming to an end very soon. I now had a little over 1,250 hours logged.

CHAPTER TWELVE

The Last Operation and Beyond

Operations on 1 May were cancelled due to the weather conditions. Despite some brief earlier signs to the contrary, the English winter had not yet released its grip on the rural Midlands and strong winds on the ground made flying nearly impossible. Chris and Bertie were on the operation to bomb Kiel the following night. It would be their first and last visit to that devastated city; though with snow showers in the morning and the possibility of thundery activity in the area in the afternoon and early evening, operations were never certain until close to take-off time. Despite this it was still a pretty busy day for Bertie. He spent some forty-five minutes in the Link trainer in the morning and had done a twenty-five-minute NFT with Chris in KB 541 before he started out on his final operational flight over Germany. There were to be sixteen Mosquitos from 163 Squadron on the raid, dispatched in two waves.

We were in the second wave that departed just before 21.30 hrs; the first wave, seven in all, had left almost an hour earlier. Chris and I were the last but one aircraft ever to lift off from Wyton's runway on a bombing operation. Only KB 624 with F/O Rowe and Sgt Newton aboard were behind us on take-off. We were timed off at 22.26 hrs and back at 02.08 hrs with Rowe and Newton in

KB 624 returning a mere ten minutes behind us. When they shut their engines down a few minutes later, 163 Squadron's and RAF Wyton's war was over.

Again there was no opposition at all on the way to Kiel; even the searchlights were very few and far between and all sixteen aircraft got back safely. I can remember thinking some time later that it was somehow fitting that both the first and last operations of 163 Squadron should be causalty free. The crews of KB 411 and KB 623 reported that they had seen the odd isolated searchlight, but that was the sum total of the German activity for the night. They would get no complaints on that score from us. Several crews saw two of the Halifaxes of 199 Squadron explode and go down in flames following a mid-air collision but overall it was not a bad night over the target. The initial climb out had been on instruments as we scrabbled through the clouds to reach our cruise altitude. Later in the night conditions had changed very little for our return to Wyton and again we had to work our way back to base on the plane's instruments. We later learned that two days after our visit the German army had fled from Kiel and that British and Canadian troops had entered the city. I can remember saying to Chris a few days after the raid that they must have been close enough to see it all happening in front of them as they approached along the roads towards the battered, smoking city.

Even before the Kiel raid, rumour was rife that the Russian army was already in the centre of Berlin and that 163 Squadron, and in fact the whole of Bomber Command, would not be going there again. Most of the area between the North Sea coast and Berlin was in Allied hands, so there were fewer and fewer targets for anyone to attack. As it turned out Kiel was the last for 163 Squadron. The crews at Wyton did not know that yet and operations were planned and then cancelled, whether for operational reasons or because the weather was quite appalling for the time of year they were never quite sure. Over those few days Wyton got drizzle, heavy rain, snow, low cloud and cold winds, sometimes on the same day. Somehow they did not miss the flying.

Within the same week the rumour mill started up again regarding victory celebrations, the fate of the Nazi leaders, new postings for the crews and all sorts of wild possibilities for the future. Then on 6 May some semblance of truth permeated the rumour network. From Bomber Command came the message that VE Day and VE+1 (8 and 9 May) would be rest days and all personnel, save a small skeleton staff chosen at the station commander's discretion, would be given time off. On hearing this, Tommy Broom headed for the mess; for once he had to work hard to get there first. There was a delegation of Russian colonels visiting the station at the time and they too joined the celebrations with great enthusiasm. This particular part of the VE celebrations at Wyton were being recorded on film and by still photography 'for the record' – others said it was to be held for future evidence!

All sorts of celebrations just happened, planned or not. A six-a-side football competition was organized, including a team of WAAFs; this was followed by an enthusiastic sing-song in the NAAFI. A mock gallows with a hung effigy of Adolf Hitler, Mussolini and the Japanese Emperor Hirohito was erected outside the officers' mess; these were later to be centre of attention as a large bonfire was lit in the evening to add to the festivities. Several local farmers also lost haystacks that night as they seemed an irresistible target for victory revellers. Flags of all colours and of all the Allied nations were produced from attics and cellars and all the local towns became a mass of red white and blue. Extra rations were sent out and distributed to the old and infirm in local retirement homes and a local brewery celebrated the event by concocting a 'Victory Brew'. There appears to be no surviving record of what it tasted like.

At 09.30 that morning the station commander made a tannoy announcement that gave all personnel not required for essential duties over the next forty-eight hours leave to go where they wished and to do what they wished. Visitors later that day included AVM Don Bennett and G/Cpt. Dixie Dean, who accompanied W/Cdr Ivor Broom as he mixed and celebrated with his squadron. The hard working ground crews, particularly the crew chiefs, had the difficult decision of catching up on a large quota of sleep or heading for the bar to join the celebrations. It is believed that in most cases a sensible compromise between the two was the option of choice.

163 Squadron had been sired out of 128 Squadron and this made Wyton a close-knit station. With the squadron commander, squadron navigation officer and several of the crews having served on both squadrons, it was inevitable that the celebrations would be a similarly combined operation. They had a history of jokes and leg-pulling between squadrons, and the outbreak of peace would not curtail that in the slightest.

Our first job of peacetime had a mixed reception. All flying was cancelled for three days, though for 163 Squadron an exception had been made so that we could exchange our old Canadian-built Mk XXVs for Mk XVIs. It was a really short trip as the new Mk XVIs were only just 8 miles down the road at RAF Upwood. We would deliver the old and return with the new, it was as simple as that. Well at least that was the theory. On the down-wind leg, just after take-off I glanced down and saw one of the leading Mosquitos 'buzzing' the airfield in general and the control tower in particular. It seemed a reasonable idea to me and a way to thank the boys and girls who were starting to emerge from all sorts of places on the airfield to watch the fun. It obviously appealed to a few more of the chaps as I was only fourth or fifth in the queue of planes to have a shot at this new sport. We didn't think we had taken too long over this, so we flew off to Upwood to collect our new planes – or so we thought.

As I pulled into a dispersal bay under a marshaller's

control I noticed a lot of gold braid on the caps of what I thought was a rather imposing welcoming committee. It didn't turn out quite that way. Having handed over the papers for our old aircraft, and got a signature, we were ushered into a crew bus and placed in a large crew room for well over an hour until A/Cdr Boyce [Senior Air Staff Officer, 8 Group] entered. He advised us of his extreme displeasure at the unauthorized display at Wyton and that we had embarrassed AVM Bennett, who had authorized the flying dispensation and also let down our squadron commander. He was pleased we had survived the war but now that we had, he did not wish to lose any of us due to unauthorized high-jinks. We were therefore to be grounded immediately and returned by road to Wyton for suitable punishment, organised by our CO, Ivor Broom.

The only reason it was not taken further up the RAF chain of command was because, when he had visited RAF Wyton, *en route* from Huntingdon and interviewed officers, airmen and WAAFs, including the air traffic officers in the tower, not one of them had seen the registration marks on any of the aircraft and the miscreants could not be positively identified!

Ivor's punishment was a week of clearing the remnants of war from the airfield, with tractors and trucks provided. Duties started between 9 o'clock and 9.30, stopped for a couple of hours at about midday while lunch and a few pints were consumed, then resumed at about 2 or 2.30 and concluded at 5 o'clock, so that the crews could make themselves ready for dinner in the mess later in the evening. A few days later Bertie collected one of the Mk XVIs from Upwood. In the interim, the Oxford was 163's only aircraft!

Over the next couple of weeks I did a few air tests and NFTs, and a forty-five-minute session in the Link practising oval orbits. In reality that was about it and the

125

⌐ down. We were told, however, that
⌐n be getting a Lancaster bomber and
⌐ng our ground crew, support staff
⌐n sightseeing tours over France and
⌐cknamed 'Cook's Tours'.
⌐ arrived on the 21st and Ivor was checked out
⌐mpared to the Mossie it was a big bird; I
⌐er standing under its wings and staring for
⌐l minutes at it, just contemplating it sheer bulk.
⌐e was no conversion training with it, you just sat for
⌐vhile with Ivor or one of the chaps he had checked out
⌐imself and he signed you off when he thought you were
sufficiently proficient not to damage it.

I did my first real 'Cook's Tour' on 28 May in a Mk XVI
Mosquito PF 507. It lasted nearly three hours, and the
devastation to the German cities, seen in daylight, was
awesome. The next day I took PF 515 and with F/O Lee
and Cpl Turner on board did a three-and-a-quarter-hour
tour of Germany. (One sat in the navigator's seat, other
in the bomb aiming position.) We flew a different route
and saw different cities, but the pattern of devastation
was the same. I also got to do several cross-county
training exercises that month, including one at night and
one over France. It was a change to relax and to see the
countryside lit up and not simply to head towards something that was burning in the distance.

On my flying assessment certificate, Form 414 (A),
issued on 2 June, Ivor noted my piloting abilities as
above the average; I was chuffed that having achieved
that rating at Hooton Park, now a year or more on, I had
managed to retain it.

My third real 'Cook's Tour' would not be until July
and as it turned out, my only flight for the month of June
would be another French cross country exercise. F/O
Robb and I spent three hours stooging around over
northern France and basically flying for pure enjoyment.
It made a real change. It had been dreadful weather in

the morning with heavy rain, though the met man got it right and we were able to head off in improving weather later in the day.

I then went back home to Norwich on leave for a few weeks.

My first trip when I got back to Wyton on a balmy late spring day was another 'Cook's Tour' over Germany in PF 515, with F/Lt Gee and Sgt Lewis on board. We were airborne for just over three and a half hours. Following an aborted bombing practice flight with Sgt Lewis on the 3rd, I then had a memorable flight with Ivor Broom in the 'new' Lancaster as a sort of second pilot, on a five hour and ten minute 'Cook's Tour' marathon with a full complement of our ground crew who had worked so hard maintaining our Mosquitos. As we overflew Cologne we were able to see the twin spires of the cathedral still standing tall amid the utter devastation that was the remains of the city.

For the next couple of weeks the weather was generally rather good, although some persistent mist and generally poor visibility put paid to very much flying. Chris and I resumed practice exercises both day and night and another 'Cook's Tour' of north Germany on the 20th. Then on the 23rd I started and completed my conversion on to the Lancaster with F/O Farfan, a black pilot from Trinidad. I managed one hour of dual in a non-dual-control Lanc over the lunch hour, while everyone else was in the mess. I was then considered 'checked out' on the huge bomber and fit to fly it on 'Cook's Tours'. Sadly my posting orders to Canada arrived at the squadron office before I ever got the chance.

However about this time I did get to fly with Tommy Broom as my navigator. More accurately I acted as pilot while Tommy used the Gee system and his superb navigational experience to assist in checking a captured German radar installation. To get it right the inbound aircraft (us) had to pinpoint its position with accuracy and confidence. The man for the job could only be Tommy. Even so the Gee set in the Mosquito was working overtime all the way. In a way this trip was supposed to help even the score of trips undertaken by the 'Flying Brooms'. Earlier in the war Ivor had made an extra trip by standing in for F/O Neal, who had twisted his ankle one night just before take off. Ivor stepped into the breach while Tommy, not knowing what was happening at the airfield, was happily elsewhere enjoying a date with a WAAF. This left the Berlin tally as follows: Ivor 22 trips; Tommy 21 trips; Bertie 19 trips. Despite his best efforts, Tommy could never persuade Ivor to allow him the additional trip to draw level again.

By now postings were almost a weekly if not daily affair. New pilots and navigators were arriving from the training and conversion units, and existing squadron personnel were getting their orders and heading off to pastures new. W/O Foggo was posted to 16 OTU as an instructor, which caused the odd chuckle and some leg-pulling in the crew room as he had just recently had the misfortune to have the first accident of peacetime. He had overshot the end of the runway at RAF Stratford and damaged his Mosquito quite a bit. Planes from 163 used to go to Stratford to allow the operators of the new ground controlled approach system (GCA) there to practise guiding Mosquitos to within a few feet of the runway. It had a much greater accuracy than the old SBA (Standard Beam Approach) system. In the same batch of postings that day Bertie was assigned to the Aircrew Holding Unit, Morecambe for transatlantic ferry duties. A very few weeks after that, almost as quickly as it had been formed, 163 Squadron was disbanded. Ivor went to Group, Chris went to 139 Squadron, and Tommy Broom went back to 'civvy street'. It was the end of an era for them all.

Bertie was at Morecambe for less than a fortnight, waiting for space on a ship to take him back to Canada. It was not a long wait in the overall scheme of things and on 12 August, along with hundreds of fellow Canadian servicemen and women, including several from Theodore, he was on board the SS *Duchess of Richmond*. It was a pleasant crossing to Halifax that took a week to complete. The week passed very quickly; it was obvious that many people were finding it hard to accept that the war was really over. During the summer months of 1945 delays in getting across the Atlantic had been greatly exacerbated by the sheer volume of American servicemen and women desperately attempting to leave Europe and get back to their homes.

The war in the east was still raging with great ferocity and the hundreds of Mosquitos produced by de Havilland Canada were needed to help defeat Japan. The plan was that the ferry unit at Dorval would fly these new planes across to England, where they would be modified for their duties in the Far East; then another ferry unit would take them onward to their forward operating squadrons. When the *Enola Gay* dropped the atomic bomb on Hiroshima on 6 August and its sister B29 dropped its bomb on Nagasaki on the 8th it changed everything totally. Before Bertie and his newly assembled colleagues had even arrived at Dorval, the reason for their going had already been assigned to history. Except for some action in Burma, there was no longer a war in the East.

The authorities in Dorval did not know what to do with ten ex-operational Mosquito crews who were not of a mind to listen to lectures by folks who through no fault of their own, had no operational experience, had never been shot at and knew less about the Mosquito than they did. It was a difficult situation. After a short while they were advised there was no longer room for them to stay at Dorval, so they would be expected to find accommodation in Montreal. Once the offer of an extra seven dollars a day was confirmed they did not hesitate and soon found themselves apartments within their means. They were expected to travel to Dorval daily to see if there was anything for them to do. As there seldom was they soon devised a system that allowed just one to go and sign everyone in. It worked well. They were then free to enjoy all that Montreal had to offer, especially the steaks at Limey Jacks, and the speakeasies for late night entertainment. They also ran into a little local difficulty with some of the French-speaking citizens, who used the pretext of asking for a light as a prelude to being a nuisance and letting forth with a tirade of abuse. Following a discussion at camp a couple of them met their match one evening and were left unconscious on the pavement. The airmen were never troubled again.

This easy life could not last and we were eventually posted to North Bay, where we were able to keep current and practise instrument flying on the radio range beams that criss-crossed almost all of the USA and Canada. It was there I earned my green card, which would be the equivalent of a modern full instrument rating. For some reason I never fully appreciated the value of what I had and it was not until later that I realized how valued it was among both RAF and commercial pilots alike. For the next three months I did a reasonable amount of flying in an assortment of aircraft, mainly of course the dear old Mossie. I flew Mk XXVIs, Mk XXIXs and a Mk III.

As P2, I also got a ferry trip in a Dakota and one all too brief air test in a Hudson. I did also have one extremely amusing interlude with a retained instructor who took a bit of a dislike to my version of single-engined approach and landing technique. I liked to have a good bit of height and speed in hand with any asymmetric manoeuvre. I explained that there was no point in flying a bad-weather circuit on one engine in perfect con-ditions. He proceeded to explain that he preferred me to approach low and slow and drag it in on the one remaining good engine. I totally disagreed but confirmed that I would be happy to demonstrate my competence at that technique if he so wished. He did.

Ten minutes later we were making a very shallow approach to low level, just as he had requested. I noticed out of the corner of my eye that he was by now starting to look more and more uncomfortable as the airfield got closer and closer and the belt of trees between us and the runway started to look higher than we were. When we reached the trees we were flying very quickly as I had let the speed build up during the approach and at the very last moment converted that speed into height and sailed easily over the trees to land gently on North Bay's tarmac runway. By then my non-combatant instructor was speaking quietly but incoherently, though I was able to distinguish the words 'mad', 'insane' and 'dangerous' from amongst his disjointed mutterings. I distinctly got the impression he was not happy, though I did try to placate him by reminding him that if he had bothered to look at the air speed indicator he would have noticed that I was allowing the speed to increase to enable me to complete the landing in total safety. He had not noticed this and what's more he obviously had no intention whatsoever of listening to my explanation. When he was eventually able to string more than a few words together coherently he announced that the senior instructor would be taking me for a full test of my competence as he did not feel that I was fit to fly. Less than half an hour into that test my assessor, S/Ldr Stevens, who had travelled with us back to Canada on the *Duchess of Richmond* turned to me and said, 'You little bastard! That's enough. Home.' Amazingly my assessment as a pilot when I left North Bay was still rated at above average. Obviously my earlier run-in with my instructor had not blighted my career.

I moved to No. 6 Ferry Unit at Dorval [now Aeroport International P-E Trudeau de Montreal] and started ferrying delightful brand new Mosquitos on the two hour trip between there and London, Ontario. It was great fun. I was flying a superb plane in uncongested skies over vast areas of picturesque Canadian forest and farmland with no one firing bullets or ack-ack shells at me. Not only that, I was getting paid for it; what more could I ask for? The weather at that time of year was kind and there was never any real pressure.

Each flight was a wonderful sightseeing trip. I took off from Dorval, usually headed straight out over the St Lawrence and followed the river on a south-westerly course towards the area known as the 'Land of a Thousand Lakes' and the vast majestic waters of Lake Ontario. Then for just over an hour I followed its forest-covered coastline towards Toronto and Lake Erie before setting course for London and its nearby airfield. Occasionally I'd take the more direct overland route from Toronto and cover the last half hour of the trip following the main railway line over the Ontario farm-lands, watching the huge Canadian Pacific locomotives hauling long winding freight carriages behind them. It was on one of these trips that I went to Brantford and renewed my friendship with the Bonney family who had moved there from Theodore. My old school chum Charlie Bonney had enlisted in the Canadian navy and we spent an agreeable hour or two comparing wartime experiences.

Whichever way I went I started to have fleeting but re-occurring thoughts of returning to Canada after the RAF had decided it no longer needed my services. I had never wanted to leave Canada in the first place, but circum-stances had dictated that I should. However, like any chap in his early twenties, any thoughts about the future were not that coherent or finalized. I had a deep love of Canada, yet I was still a serving RAF officer with lots of wonderful aeroplanes to fly. As it was a decision I did not have to make just yet, I could settle back and enjoy the flying; or so I thought. It lasted less than a month before I received my orders to return home, and I had done less than a dozen ferry trips and no transatlantic crossings. That was a real shame; I had really started to enjoy my time in Canada. I was starting to feel like a real Canadian again. But on 26 November 1945, I clambered aboard a bright, shiny B 24 Liberator operated by BOAC and returned to Prestwick. We were airborne for eleven hours with a one-and-a-half-hour refuelling stopover at Gander in Newfoundland. I well remember how noisy it was and how glad I felt that I had got to fly the dear old Mossie rather than one of these things.

I was posted to 1409 Met Flight at Lyneham in Wiltshire, and unsurprisingly my first flight there on 4 January 1946 was an air test. My navigator was F/Sgt Derek Spinks. Derek and I would fly together for the next six months. Like Jim Churcher and Chris Hart before them, with Derek I was assigned a super crew mate; another calm, reliable, dependable chap I could always rely on 100 per cent. Like Jim he was much taller than me, but somehow we managed to co-ordinate our walking abilities so that we arrived at the aircraft at round about the same time. That made a change, I can tell you. Over the next three months we did a lot of flying over France, usually turning over Marseilles and Toulouse when we reached the Mediterranean coast at dawn. In January and February the beaches of the northern Mediterranean coast looked almost inviting when occasionally bathed in early morning winter sunshine, compared to our cold and often gloomy winter weather back at Lyneham.

No. 1409 Met Flight had been based at Wyton as part of 8 Group. Now it had been moved to Lyneham it operated in the same role for the whole of Transport Command and would continue to do so until communications and weather-reporting facilities became more normal after the disruption of war. All this meant more work for the navigator, for now as well as his navigating duties he had the responsibility of noting weather conditions and cloud formations throughout the trip and reporting the observations upon his return to Lyneham. There was a telephone hook-up available so that he would also be reporting to Transport Command,

Overseas Air Command and three or four other organizations with responsibilities for post-war weather forecasting.

No. 1409 had this regular run to the south of France and nothing was allowed to get in the way of it taking place. We took off in rain, hail, mist and even snow storms. We had to be overhead Marseilles at dawn, which meant that as spring approached and we moved from January to March, and as the mornings got lighter, so we had to set off earlier and earlier for our five-hour journey to arrive at the Mediterranean at the correct time. It also meant that I logged two hours of night flying every trip. The map reference of the position where we dropped down to sea level was 4450N and 0030E. We took temperature and barometric pressure as we descended. By the time we reached Perpignon it was time to climb back to our normal operational height of 25,000 feet for the flight home. As a flight sergeant, Derek's accommodation was in the sergeants' mess at Lyneham; while we commissioned pilots lived off camp in a large requisitioned country house some 5 or 6 miles from the airfield. This all sounded very grand until it came to getting to the airfield very early on cold, frosty winter mornings. We were provided with a 10 horsepower Hillman van with a canvas back and a 15 hundredweight Bedford truck also with a canvas rear cover. Neither were wonderful starters and we had to learn the idiosyncrasies of them both. It was also the pilot's job to make sure he got up in time to do this and get to the aircraft on time, having collected his navigator on the way. At 4 a.m., there was not much activity at Lyneham and none at all at the billets. The Hillman was the preferred mode of transport, but more often that not it refused to start. As the starter on the Bedford would never engage, it was frequently down to cranking the brute. This was a mighty hazardous operation as it kicked like a mule and the crank handle had to be held just so, or it could break the operators thumb. It always eventually started, but what intrepid aviators we felt after this when taking off into a snowstorm!

We were down in the Bay of Biscay on 23 January in very severe weather. It was the first time I had experienced such massive towers of cumulo-nimbus clouds. I could see underneath them and it looked as if there were corridors between them, all very enticing but not for us. It looked spectacular as we passed over it at 38,000 feet.

On 2 February we headed out to 4610N, 16W, midway across the Atlantic. That seemed a lonely place and a long way from home, especially long for F/O 'Percy' Vere, who a few days later had to coax his plane back on one engine after the other failed at the turning point. I remember how pleased and relieved he was when he landed at Lyneham.

Returning from the Marseilles run one February morning, we ran into fog in the Paris area. I increased manifold pressure and reduced the RPM to achieve the most economical cruise settings. Over the Isle of Wight I called Lyneham, who promptly advised that we divert to St Mawgan. I knew Lyneham was equipped with GCA, and as I had practised making GCA approaches on almost every flight that I had flown, I knew the operators and they knew me. I advised the controller at Lyneham that we had plenty of fuel to divert to St Mawgan and asked permission to do a practice GCA approach. It was thick fog at ground level and the GCA approach had been perfect; so I landed. I then taxied in at a snail's pace and stopped by the control tower. Derek gathered up his bag with the annotated map and walked into the tower to see his met man and report on the telephone hook-up. At first they didn't believe he was the chap who had left in the middle of the night on the met flight, but eventually they did.

There was an inquiry relating to this landing in fog. I said that I had done exactly what I was told and when the GCA operator advised 'Threshold', Derek shouted 'Lights' and I throttled back. Later Derek told me he did not see any lights, so I must have. Such is the working of the human brain.

In April, Derek and I were transferred to 162 Squadron at Blackbushe, which was responsible for diplomatic mail and inter-embassy communications. As Derek cheerfully noted, 'We've made it at last Bertie – I always wanted to be a ruddy postman!' And to be truthful, that's what we were. Having said that we had some fun in the process, as we had moved to another 'flying club' where we already knew a lot of the chaps. We started flying to countries we had never even been to before, delivering dark blue bags of diplomatic mail, and we got to have a few very enjoyable overnight stops into the bargain. None of this rush there and back on the same day routine any more. It was all a really civilized way of life. Ironically we even got to go to Germany almost a year to the day after my last operation to Kiel. This time it was to deliver newspapers to Guttersloh, over a quiet and peaceful Europe. A couple of days later we headed east towards Prague, stopped there overnight and then went south to Vienna and another overnight stop before heading back home. This more or less became the pattern of life for the next three months. Rome and Naples were soon added to the list of regular stopping points. It became a very agreeable way of earning a living.

Despite the fun he was having, Bertie was starting to think that he could do more for the reconstruction of England and Europe by turning his hand to industry. So after several weeks of thinking and weighing up his options, he decided that the lure of the outside world outweighed the benefits of staying in the RAF. On 3 July he was posted to No. 1 Ferry Unit (FU) RAF Pershore. Thirteen flights later, on the 31st he flew his last trip for the RAF. Fittingly it was in a Mk VI Mosquito. With F/O Watson as navigator he ferried NT 198 to Chateau-Dun, a small airfield to the south-west of Paris and then cadged a lift back to Blackbushe in a Lancaster. Until his discharge on 6 November he remained at 1FU Pershore, counting the days off until he became a civilian once more. At Pershore there were no further opportunities to fly and he also spent quite a while in various hospitals with a severe bout of double pneumonia and a quick visit to the surgeon to have his tonsils removed. He had been plagued with a bout of tonsillitis almost every winter since boyhood and this seemed a good opportunity to solve it once and for all.

After he left Pershore he would have to supply his own plane and pay for his own flying.

CHAPTER THIRTEEN

Flying For Fun

A truck was hired to collect the bits. When it turned into the Boulter drive many hours and many hundreds of miles later, it contained most of the parts of a rather unique aeroplane, Boeing Stearman PT 17, USAAC number 40-1766. Initially registered as N52061 and later to become N8162G, this Stearman was to prove rather special to Bertie, once he got to know it. Complete with a Continental R-670-5 radial engine that was fitted with pistons and barrels from a Sherman tank engine, and enough bits (almost) to rebuild the plane to flying condition, it was now his. It would become a three-year project for Bertie, now in the first flush of full retirement. Strictly speaking the engine was not on the truck at that stage, as it had already been dropped off at Eastern Stearman, some twenty minutes earlier on the way home. There was, however, still a vast collection of boxes of bits and pieces piled up on the floor of the truck. All would need to find a home in the double garage at the side of the Boulter home in Saxlingham Nethergate. It was late 1991.

But all this is jumping the gun a bit. I first thought about getting myself a Stearman some time earlier, probably in the summer of 1989 or 1990. But as you well know, the home, the family, business, and all the sorts of things that come with them, have a much higher priority at the time than rebuilding an old aeroplane. I had regained my civilian licence at Shipdham airfield during 1989 and was happily spending my spare time flying the usual range of planes found in a typical rural English flying club.

I had renewed my membership with the Pathfinder Association, having attended a couple of its functions at the Dorchester in the late forties and early 1950s and then let things drift. I had rejoined as retirement beckoned and spare time became more available (at least in theory) and Christine [Bertie's wife] and I travelled to London to attend one of the last Pathfinder balls held at one of the Park Lane hotels. Both our daughters, Sarah and Deborah, along with their husbands David and Nigel, wanted to come, and I wanted them to meet some of my old contemporaries.

Needless to say we were seated well away from the top table. During one of the dances that followed the meal, Chris and I passed close behind Ivor and I couldn't resist singing 'Too Ra Loo Ra Laylee. Too Ra Loo Ra Lie' so that he could hear. The reaction from Ivor was electric, he stopped dancing and wheeled round and boomed 'Bertie the Boy', and in an instant a friendship that had been on hold for several decades was reborn. [Too Ra Loo Ra Laylee was the section of an Irish lullaby that Ivor would sing briefly on the radio to confirm to the squadron that he had completed the raid and was passing 3 degrees east and safely on his way home.] The looks on Christine's, Sarah's and Deborah's faces were something to behold when a real live knighted air marshal came to our table to meet them and to find out all about the family. Ivor naturally brought Lady Jess with him and another friendship was started. There was to be another ball the following year. Before they left Ivor gave me my instructions (no change there, then). 'You will attend with all your family and you will be on my table.'

Ivor was president of the association at the time, and on his table the following year were Ly Bennett, widow of the Pathfinders' founder, Don Bennett and Diana

Searby, the widow of the famed Pathfinder master bomber, John Searby. It was a fabulous evening amidst great and illustrious company. This friendship with Ivor continued until his death in 2003. Chris and I were on holiday in Cape Town when we heard the sad news. It was with great pride that at Lady Jess's request I carried Ivor's medals and decorations to the altar at the RAF Church of St Clement Danes at Ivor's memorial thanksgiving service. How lucky I was to have Tommy Broom on my left and John Brown on my right as I took that solemn walk.

About the time I rejoined the Pathfinder Association I also became a member of the Arnold Scheme Register. This came about as a result of joining the Aircrew Association, whose organizers had passed my name to Norman Bates, who had started the Register. He seemed genuinely excited that I was still alive and delighted that I was very interested in what he was doing tracing all the aircrew who had been involved with the Arnold Scheme all those years ago. In that first conversation Norman mentioned that Ron Gould had organized a get-together and they were meeting at Old Buckenham airfield the following Sunday and that a chap named Jim Avis had got a few Stearmans there. We went along and on 14 September 1991 I was bitten by the Stearman bug again. A short while earlier ex-RAF ferry pilot David Backhouse and his Stearman had got involved with Jim Avis. The result of this association had led to thirteen of the fourteen of the ex- Arnold Scheme cadets who were there for the barbecue, getting to fly a PT17 again. That particular plane was soon to be Jim's new toy, but that is a separate story. Considering that we were all well into our late middle age, we should have known better; I certainly didn't. Ten seconds after take off I knew that N3922B had me totally hooked again.

I went to see Jim again a couple of weeks later, this time at Swanton Morley, when I got my second chance to fly the plane. It was delightful, and it all came flooding back – well enough that when we landed Jim said, 'Good enough for me Bertie. You are up to solo standard again. I'll phone you.' I was not so sure, I still had less than an hour of refamiliarization time on the Stearman and Darr Aero Tech was over half a lifetime ago. But Jim was the instructor, so I did as I was told. On 6 October I met him and the Stearman at the grass airfield at Swanton Morley and of course he was right. I did know what I was doing and I did have fun. The thirty-five minutes logged that day went past in a flash. It was simply superb. I had soloed in a real PT17 again, a first since 1942. I felt nineteen years old again.

A few months after going solo, as the spring of 1992 brought with it some decent flying weather, I was able to introduce Christine and the children to the joys of flying in a Stearman. Those flights, I have to tell you, produced some of the most joyful experiences of my life, ranking alongside marrying Chris and the birth of our children. It was certainly something I would never have dreamed of all those years ago in the dark days of the war.

Within a month or so from that first flight Jim asked Christine whether she meant it when she told him she thought that I would like to own a Stearman. A few days later he pulled me to one side and told me he had located an unfinished Stearman project languishing in a barn on an old army camp somewhere 'down south'. For £25,000 cash I would get enough bits to reassemble a PT17 to flying condition. Was I interested? He estimated that a further £15,000 would be needed and after that I would have one of the most pristine examples of the marque available. He really was totally convincing and I took it on face value. However, not everything he had been told about the plane and its condition was correct, although he was certainly right about it being unfinished.

We were not aware at that stage that it was an ex-Darr Aero Tech plane that we were looking at, but nevertheless it seemed too good an opportunity to miss. When we arrived at its temporary home in Gloucestershire it looked in a pretty sorry state. Sure the frame had been restored, but that was about all. The seats were definitely not from a Stearman, the whole wiring loom was shot, the seat belts were useless and of the instrument panel, only the combined pressure and temperature gauge was known to work. If that part of it was in a mess then the rest was in an even worse condition. We elected to leave behind bits that were either too far gone or simply not of Stearman origin, and this included the engine-mounting frame with cracked welds and tubes.

The PT17 had been a crop duster in one of its former lives. Between Bertie's first introduction to it as a primary trainer in the early 1940s and owning it in the early 1990s a lot had happened to it, not all good. A lot of crop-dusting bits and pieces that were not needed came in the crate along with the bits that they actually did want, and the smell from the pesticides permeated throughout the boxes and everything within a 10 foot radius of it. It took some sorting to get things segregated, as there seemed little order or logic to the contents of the boxes. However from the paperwork in one box they were able to trace its history from manufacture, through its military career during the war years, to its civilian life in North America, and then on down to Central America, where it apparently had a long and successful life as a crop sprayer. There was no disguising that, and the distinctive smell of its past occupation hung around the workshop for months.

I had dropped the engine in to the Eastern Stearman works of Jim Avis as we were heading home. I vividly recall one of his first expressions when he saw the contents of the van. 'It'll need a big fix,' he said; he was not wrong. Jim was one of the top men in Europe involved in Stearman restoration at the time, so who was I to doubt him? Not surprisingly it would be nearly three long years and quite a bit of cash before No. 28 would take to the skies again, this time over the flat farmlands of Norfolk. Along with all the time needed to do the restoration came a lot of the traditional blood, sweat and tears that are all part of any major restoration project. They would be shed in full measure on No. 28 before that first flight happened. As Jim dismantled the engine, I started the inspection of the crates of bits during the daytime and Christine helped me as I started combing through the pile of aircraft paperwork late on during the evenings after supper. Cleaning, checking, restoring and repainting would occupy the next year and it would be March 1993 before full-scale rebuilding would commence.

Despite the pressure this put on our time, we made sure that we found the time to return to Canada on a regular basis. Our visits back to Theodore continued, and life-long friendships were maintained and grew. However pleasant these all too brief interludes were, however, there was always the Stearman awaiting us on our return. By now we had pieced together its story.

No. 28 had indeed come a long way. Built by Boeing at their Wichita plant in mid-1940, it was commissioned by the army on 17 July of that year and assigned to the Spartan School of Aeronautics in Tulsa, Oklahoma. For reasons that could never be established, just three month later, on 7 October, it was transferred to my old Arnold Scheme training establishment in Albany, Darr Aero Tech.

As far as we can tell it survived fairly well as a primary trainer until 9 August the following year, when an English cadet named Ray H. Nelson did it a fair amount of damage when he struck one of the airport boundary markers on the Darr Aero site. We believe it was repaired locally and put back into service for a short while until it was badly damaged again, in a wind storm that hit the Albany airfield on 27 January 1942. This time it was too much for the local ground crews to put right in the time they had available, so it was derigged and sent to the Orlando base of Florida Aircraft Inc., who were contracted to the Army Air Corps to provide repair and maintenance services. It was definitely the repair side of the operation that was needed on this occasion. Once fully repaired it returned to Darr Aero Tech and served there more or less uneventfully until 20 December 1944. It was on its return from Florida Aircraft in June and July of 1942 that I must have first flown in it. I seem to recall that we flew everything that was parked on the line in those days. You simply took whichever Stearman was assigned to you and off you went. There was no record to relate flight line numbers to aircraft serial numbers, so I cannot say on which day or on which training exercise I flew in it during that long summer, but certainly I must have flown in it some time during my stay in Albany.

Six months or so after I left Darr Aero Tech for Cochran Field and the Vultee, it was reassigned to the Southern Airways Flying School, located 250 miles north in Decatur, Alabama, close to the Tennessee border. By the time of this move, the records show it had logged 2,068.9 hours, mainly at the hands of unskilled, ham-fisted, *ab initio* pilots like me. It was certainly a tough working plane, as those hours and the previous incidents will testify. It stayed in the hands of the AAC training programme until the second of July; several weeks after the war in Europe had finished.

On 2 July 1945 it was handed over to the Reconstruction Finance Corporation and sold off as army surplus, almost certainly at one of the huge government surplus sales auctions conducted on the municipal airport 5 or 6 miles to the north-west of Birmingham, Alabama. The next notable phase of its history was to be reregistered as a civilian aircraft as it came off the US Army inventory and on to the civilian register. So reregistered as N52061 it went to back to work training pilots at a civilian flight school in Jacksonville in Florida.

Seven years later it was converted into a single-seat crop duster with 'ag and pest' certifications before it was flown to Central America, where it was to work in agricultural aviation for the next thirty or so years. Whilst in El Salvador it was returned to its two-seater configuration and the hopper was removed, though by whom and under what authorization they could never find out. In early 1989 it was flown back to the USA in a totally unairworthy state by Robert McAfee and remained based in Georgia for a while, where it appeared to change owners a few times as its condition deteriorated still further. At this stage it was put back on to the American register as N8162G.

When the plane had crossed the border between the USA and Mexico on the way to El Salvador all those years ago, the paperwork trail become rather sketchy to the point of being non-existent. Crop dusting was an industry with a history of being fairly relaxed, informal and not prone to vast amounts of red tape and forms. In the early 1950s that was particularly noticeable. By then the profession had attracted a rather high proportion of independently minded ex-military flyers, recently let off their leashes and now operating in the countries of South and Central America, where avoiding what little red tape there was had already become a national pastime. The moment it left the United States the paperwork trail did not just go cold, it froze. That is until some time after its return to the USA in 1989 and its subsequent rebirth in England.

Once the long careful process of strip-down started it became clear that the frame was pretty much all right. There were a few tubes that had been replaced in obvious positions of any plane with a crop dusting history, all well documented with photographs, but other than that it was fine and the repaint made it look as good as new. The task was to make all the other bits airworthy and look compatible with the frame – not as simple a task as it sounds. The wings were a totally different story from the frame. When the upper wings were dismantled they revealed very heavy corrosion on a great deal of the internal structural components, so bad that many individual parts were beyond salvage and needed total replacement. Then when the lower wings were looked at, Bertie and the engineers were amazed to find that they were in a far worse state altogether. Some of the attachment bolts were so corroded that they sheared the moment the slightest pressure was applied to undo them and even those that held were in a very poor condition. Amazingly on some the shank portion was missing altogether; it was simply a head on one side of the fixing and a nut and washer assembly on the other. To add to the problem, a few of the components were virtually corroded together into what appeared to be single solid lumps of steel or aluminium oxide. It was turning into a major nightmare.

Then there were the wheels and brakes. On the Stearman the brake drums are recessed into the lightweight magnesium alloy wheels. On the example in the Boulter workshop they were corroded solid. It would take a mixture of penetrating fluid, a brazing torch and hours and hours of patient tapping, twisting, pushing and pulling before any signs of movement were to occur on the first wheel assembly. As the days went past the size of the hammer and the quantity of penetrating fluid increased, with little effect. The heating of the mag-alloy wheels with a propane torch was one process they were particularly glad to see the back of, knowing the metal's tendency to burn happily if severely overheated. They had wrapped wet towels round the wheels as a precaution and were not very confident of the process, but they were desperate. Once the freeing-up exercise was done on one wheel, the whole process had to be repeated for the other wheel assembly. It took at least a couple of weeks to complete the work. The tail-wheel assembly was also amazing. The bearings were damaged to the point of extinction, and the rear oleo looked as if it probably had not functioned correctly for years.

It amazed us that this plane had apparently flown for some time in this condition, particularly with reference to the structural integrity of the wings. Initially they had all looked pretty reasonable when I started dismantling them. But the further we dug, the worse it looked. It did prompt us to conjecture over coffee one day on the possible quantity of other Stearmans with similar histories that may well have been still flying around. Almost certainly, we felt, with their pilots and owners blissfully ignorant of the extremely fragile condition of some of the important, structural parts of their aircraft. It was a scary thought.

The engine was obviously not the original one fitted to it by Boeing half a century earlier; the numbers simply did not match. It was, however, the same make and same model. Airframe 40-1766 had initially been fitted with a seven-cylinder Continental R-670-5 radial engine, and that was what it would eventually fly with in its rebirth in England. The one that came with it had been rebuilt in America some time earlier. This was probably immediately after its return flight from South America, when it was recorded that it made a forced landing on a road in California, following a dramatic loss of oil pressure and oil shortly after it crossed over from Mexico into America. However the rebuild was a bit basic to say the least and the cylinders were actually refugees from the engine of a Sherman tank. That in itself was no real problem as a variant of the same Continental engine was standard fit in the Sherman, save for a few extra cooling shroud studs needed on the tank variant to aid the cooling via a large fan and shroud system.

The paperwork from South America was non-existent. That covering the engine rebuild was by comparison complete, but as far as we could tell, totally fictitious. It stated that there were new ignition cables with the engine – there were not. It also stated that both magnetos and the carburettor had been fully overhauled – they had not. It confirmed that the engine had been fully bench run, after which all the valves had been shut down and the engine treated with an inhibitor. Very obviously this had never happened. How could we tell? Simple really, all the ignition wires from the magnetos had been cut through very close to the magneto body, and there were no replacements. Then, when Jim removed all the plugs and turned it over by hand, every rotation was greeted by a loud and melodious tinkle. There was a substantial metallic something floating around inside the engine! There was simply no way this engine had ever run since its 'rebuild'.

Jim's work to remove all the cylinders revealed a new gudgeon-pin cap lurking in the depths of the engine. Our immediate thought was that however impossible it seemed, it had somehow worked free from its piston and dropped into the crank case. A quick check soon revealed that this was not so. Incredibly this interloper was a spare, presumably dropped into the crank case during the reassembly – and yet the engine was still signed off as fit to fly! Obviously a full inspection of an engine with this sort of pedigree (or lack of) was going to be essential, particularly as we now also knew that it had also missed out on the process of being inhibited. Somehow by then we were not unduly surprised.

I had spent many hours sitting in a Stearman, and it was very apparent that the throttle quadrant that came with the box of bits was not of Boeing manufacture. Fortunately I had also spent an almost equal number of hours in a North American Harvard and it was easy for me to recognize that it was there that I had seen it before. 'My' Stearman throttle quadrant actually owed its origins to the advanced trainer, the Harvard AT-6. Its replacement back to original PT 17 design was added to the fast-growing list of bits needing to be located, or at worst completely remade.

The year 1993 was slipping past at an alarming rate. There were a few days when a lot of progress was made, and there were other more plentiful days when the only direction we were achieving with the project seemed to be backwards.

Despite the many backward steps in the restoration process, No. 28 was slowly being pieced back together. In the spring of 1994 when it became obvious that it was within a few months of completion, Jim Avis and I spent more and more time getting my competence in flying a Stearman back into shape. By the end of June the engine was running, the airframe was on its wheels and it was starting to look like a real aeroplane. All that was needed was the correct paperwork signed by an FAA surveyor qualified to do the job. That took place on 1 July when No. 28 got its FAA Certificate of Airworthiness as an authentic Boeing Stearman PT 17. It was the end of a long and expensive road.

On 2 July 1994, No 28. flew for the first time with Gerry Honey at the controls. After he had declared himself satisfied with its performance and handling he passed it over to Dave Bagshaw for a second opinion. Dave was of the same opinion as Gerry, No. 28 was fit to fly and was to be released to service. Jim then hopped aboard and flew it around until he too was satisfied that all was well. So later that day, after Jim had had a thorough look round between flights, he and I clambered aboard and at long last I got my first chance to fly my own plane. For forty glorious minutes Jim, N8162G and I floated around in the Norfolk skies. I have to say I had an indecently smug feeling about the whole thing; it truly was a day to savour. There was a minor setback when a small oil plug popped out of the engine and the starboard brake assembly sprang a leak, but overall it had performed exactly to the book. A late-evening shift for Jim and me solved the problems. It was ready for the rest of the world to see. The following day Jim and I flew it to the home of the Shuttleworth Collection at Old Warden for another of the Arnold Scheme reunion meetings. It looked superb standing in line with it contemporaries on the Old Warden grass, so much so that it won the award for best Stearman, a fitting reward for all that effort. It was a real proving flight there and back; two hours twenty-five in total. Just two days later Chris had her turn in our new toy and over the following weeks the rest of the family followed suit. No. 28 was now not just mine, it was fully part of our family. It was a momentous few weeks of my life that I will never forget.

Over the next eight years Bertie and No. 28 flew together between 350 to 400 times. Apart from himself and his family he also got to fly with other members of the Arnold Scheme Register, the Spitfire Association, and colleagues from 128 and 163 Squadron, Sir Ivor and Tommy Broom. Sir Ivor flew on 7 October 1994 and again on 26 July 1999. Tommy Broom on the other hand was almost an annual visitor to Swanton Morley with flights logged in May 1994, Aug 1995, May 1997 and May 1999.

By late 2001, after many years of virtually trouble-free flying it was becoming obvious that No. 28 was being be used less and less. Swanton Morley had closed and Bertie had taken up residence at Shipdham. The hangar at Shipdham was smaller than the one at Swanton, and No. 28 needed at least two people to assist with the ground handling. This was not always possible at Shipdham, as it was run by members, with no full time staff. Regretfully the decision was made to sell the Stearman and hang up the goggles and helmet (though Bertie decided that he would keep his pilot's licence, just in case something turned up from time to time – which it usually did either in the form of Martin and Vicky Shaw's Stearman or the PA 28-180 that Peter and Jane Bodle had an interest in). By now N8162G had moved to Luxemburg and was reregistered to LX-LWK as it passed into the hands of a very proud new owner, commercial pilot Wolfgang Liebler.

In his flying career Bertie had logged well over 3,000 hours in over forty different types of aircraft. He had flown in ten different countries and covered virtually everything from single-seat gliders to four-engined bombers during a career that spanned well over half a century. Now perhaps it was time to step back a little, collect his thoughts, marshal his lifetime of memories and write about it.

Aircraft Flown

de Havilland Tiger Moth DH 82A
Boeing Stearman PT 17
Vaultee Valiant BT 13A
North American Harvard AT 6A
North American Harvard AT 6C
Airspeed Oxford
Avro Anson
Blackburn Botha
Bristol Blenheim Mk V
de Havilland Mosquito Mk 111
de Havilland Mosquito Mk 1V
de Havilland Mosquito Mk XX
de Havilland Mosquito Mk XXV
de Havilland Mosquito Mk XV1
de Havilland Mosquito Mk XX1X
de Havilland Mosquito Mk V1
Percival Proctor
Avro Lancaster
Douglas Dakota
Morane Rallye
Aircoupe
Luton Minor
Piper PA 28 -140
Piper PA 28 -161
Piper PA 28 -180

de Havilland Chipmunk DHC1
Cessna 150
Cessna 152
Cessna 172-Hawke
Piper PA 34T
Piper PA 30 Twin Comanche
Aerospatiale TB 9
Piper PA 24-250

GLIDERS

T 21
Tudor
Olympia
Olympia 403
Swallow
Mieser
Cranich
Skylark 2
K6
Motor Falke
Blanik

APPENDIX TWO

Combat Operations Flown

Date	Aircraft	Navigator	Target
1944			
128 Squadron. RAF WYTON			
23 October	Mosquito XXV	Sgt Jim Churcher	Wiesbaden
24 October	Mosquito XXV	Sgt Jim Churcher	Hanover
29 October	Mosquito XXV	Sgt Jim Churcher	Cologne
1 November	Mosquito XXV	Sgt Jim Churcher	Berlin
3 November	Mosquito XVI	Sgt Jim Churcher	Berlin
4 November	Mosquito XVI	Sgt Jim Churcher	Hanover
6 November	Mosquito XVI	Sgt Jim Churcher	Gelsenkirchen
18 November	Mosquito XVI	Sgt Jim Churcher	Wanne-Eikel
21 November	Mosquito XVI	Sgt Jim Churcher	Sterkrade
25 November	Mosquito XVI	Sgt Jim Churcher	Nuremburg A/C abandoned – Dunkirk
4 December	Mosquito XVI	Sgt Jim Churcher	Hagen
6 December	Mosquito XVI	Sgt Jim Churcher	Berlin
9 December	Mosquito XVI	Sgt Jim Churcher	Berlin
11 December	Mosquito XVI	Sgt Jim Churcher	Hamborn
12 December	Mosquito XVI	Sgt Jim Churcher	Osnabruck
17 December	Mosquito XVI	Sgt Jim Churcher	Duisburg
18 December	Mosquito XVI	Sgt Jim Churcher	Jettisoned Load – North Sea
28 December	Mosquito XVI	Sgt Jim Churcher	Frankfurt
31 December	Mosquito XVI	Sgt Jim Churcher	Berlin

Date	Aircraft	Navigator	Target
1945			
1 January	Mosquito XVI	Sgt Jim Churcher	Hanover
4 January	Mosquito XVI	Sgt Jim Churcher	Berlin
5 January	Mosquito XVI	Sgt Jim Churcher	Jettisoned Load – North Sea
7 January	Mosquito XVI	Sgt Chris Hart	Nuremburg
14 January	Mosquito XVI	Sgt Chris Hart	Berlin A/C abandoned – Thurleigh

163 Squadron RAF Wyton

Date	Aircraft	Navigator	Target
8 February	Mosquito XXV	Sgt Chris Hart	Berlin
10 February	Mosquito XXV	Sgt Chris Hart	Hanover
12 February	Mosquito XXV	Sgt Chris Hart	Stuttgart
13 February	Mosquito XXV	Sgt Chris Hart	Bonn
19 February	Mosquito XXV	Sgt Chris Hart	Erfurt
20 February	Mosquito XXV	Sgt Chris Hart	Berlin
22 February	Mosquito XXV	Sgt Chris Hart	Berlin
23 February	Mosquito XXV	Sgt Chris Hart	Worms
26 February	Mosquito XXV	Sgt Chris Hart	Berlin
28 February	Mosquito XXV	Sgt Chris Hart	Berlin
1 March	Mosquito XXV	Sgt Chris Hart	Berlin
3 March	Mosquito XXV	Sgt Chris Hart	Berlin
4 March	Mosquito XXV	Sgt Chris Hart	Essen
6 March	Mosquito XXV	Sgt Chris Hart	Wesel
7 March	Mosquito XXV	Sgt Chris Hart	Munster
20 March	Mosquito XXV	Sgt Chris Hart	Bremen
21 March	Mosquito XXV	Sgt Chris Hart	Berlin
2 April	Mosquito XXV	F/O Howell	Berlin
10 April	Mosquito XXV	F/O Howell	Chemnitz
12 April	Mosquito XXV	Sgt Chris Hart	Berlin
16 April	Mosquito XXV	Sgt Chris Hart	Berlin
19 April	Mosquito XXV	Sgt Chris Hart	Schleissheim
20 April	Mosquito XXV	Sgt Chris Hart	Berlin
3 May	Mosquito XXV	Sgt Chris Hart	Kiel

Summary

48 Combat operations flown
Two a/c abandoned:. MM410 and MM204
Two operations aborted, 1 engine failure, 1 collision
128,000 lb ordnance dropped on enemy territory.

APPENDIX THREE

The Pathfinders

Don Bennett, then a Group Captain, formed the Pathfinder Force at Wyton, near Huntingdon in August 1942 with five squadrons taken from five bomber groups. They were formed as, and remained with the addition of 105 and 139 squadrons, the marker squadrons, until the end of the war in Europe.

No. 7 Squadron	Short Sterling
No. 35 Squadron	Handley Page Halifax
No. 83 Squadron	Avro Lancaster
No. 156 Squadron	Vickers Armstrong Wellington
No. 109 Squadron	Vickers Armstrong Wellington

It was evident that the Pathfinder Force needed more squadrons to back up markers, to carry out diversionary raids to draw the fighters off the mainstream heavy bombers as they approached their targets as well as to carry out independent bombing raids. Bennett soon got his additional Lancasters and Mosquitos.

In January 1943 the Pathfinder Force became a separate group, No. 8, and Don Bennett was promoted to air commodore – Air Officer Commanding No. 8(PFF) Group. He was soon promoted to air vice-marshal and was joined by Group Captain C.D.C. Boyce as Senior Air Staff Officer (SASO).

From the start of the Pathfinders' involvement, the efficiency of Bomber Command's operations improved

dramatically and the introduction of OBOE as a marking
device in December 1942 greatly improved the efficiency and
accuracy of target marking. (Such was the reputation of 8
Group to deliver, that by the end of the war it had grown to
six Lancaster squadrons, including No. 405 RCAF Squadron,
eleven Mosquito squadrons and No. 1409 Mosquito Met
Flight, based at Wyton. Additionally two Lancaster and
one Mosquito squadron were seconded to No. 5 Group.) The
Mosquito squadrons became the Light Night Striking Force.

Group Captain Hamish Mahaddie, DSO, DFC, AFC, was
appointed by Don Bennett to search for additional pilots in
other bomber groups, flying training command units, operational training units – in fact anywhere he could find pilots
with 1,000 hours' experience or more. He was extremely
persuasive in extolling the virtues of the Mosquito in particular and the Pathfinders in general, and became widely
known throughout the RAF as 'the horse thief' for his efforts.

Many of the pilots in 8 Group were battle-hardened
veterans, having survived one or even two tours of
operations, mostly on heavy bombers. Quite a few of them
already wore DFC and DSO ribbons, and were a tower of
strength and experience within their squadrons. But many
were also young men with no operational experience at all,
some being hardly out of their teens. Many were Canadians,
New Zealanders, Australians and South Africans, all fighting
far from home.

They did however all have at least two things in common;
all Pathfinder aircrew were volunteers, and all were fiercely
determined to win.

Bibliography

128 Squadron Records, Ministry of Defence, 1945
163 Squadron Records, Ministry of Defence, 1945
163 Mosquito Bomber Squadron, Barry Blunt, B. Blunt, 2002
Clean Sweep, Terry Spooner, Crecy Books, 1994
Cochran Field, Army and Navy Publications Inc. 1942
The Encyclopaedia of Military Aircraft, Robert Jackson, Parragon, 2003
Ferry Pilots' Notes, RAF Transport Command, 1944
Military Airfields in the British Isles 1939–1945, Steve Willis and Barry Holliss, Enthusiasts Publications, 1990
A Posset Lad, Tom Evans, Evans/Broom, 1999
Stearman, Jim Avis and Martin Bowman, Airlife, 1997
Theodore, Theodore Historical Society, 1987

Index

Armitage, F/O, 10
Avis, Jim, 140, 141, 142, 143, 149

Backhouse, David, 140
Bagshaw, Dave, 149
Baker, F/Lt, 119
Barr, P/O, 25
Barton, Cyril, 22
Bates, Norman, 140
Beckett, Joe, 7
Bell, P/O, 25
Bell , Sgt, 36
Bellis, John, 22
Bennett, AVM Don, 67, 99, 101, 124, 125,
    139
Bennett, Ly, 67, 139
Bishop, William, 22
Blackie, F/Sgt Gordon, 44
Bodle, Peter, 150
Bodle, Jane, 150
Boles, Sgt, 31
Bonakis, F/Lt, 44
Bonnie, Charlie, 132
Booth-Smith, Peter, 22, 24, 25
Bottom, Sgt, 31
Boulter, Annie Eliza (mother), 1, 2, 4
Boulter, Christine (wife), 139, 140, 141,
    143, 150
Boulter, Claude (father), 1, 2
Boulter , Deborah, 139
Boulter, Sarah, 139
Bowen, F/Lt, 108
Boyce, A/Cdr, 125
Boyle, W/O, 112
Broom, AM, Sir, Ivor, 50, 55, 62, 67, 86, 89,
    91, 97, 99, 100, 101, 102, 105, 109, 111,
    124, 125, 127, 128, 140, 150
Broom , Lady, Jess, 139, 140

Broom, F/Lt Tommy, 50, 55, 61, 62, 64, 82,
    86, 87.89, 91, 97, 99, 100, 101 102, 111,
    123, 126, 127, 128, 140, 150
Brown, John, 140
Buckley, S/Ldr, 46
Buxton, Herbert, 5

Churcher, Sgt Jim, 48, 49, 54, 55, 56, 58, 59,
    60, 61, 62, 63, 64, 70, 71, 72, 73, 74 75,
    78, 79, 80, 81, 82, 83, 84, 85, 90, 91, 92,
    97, 133
Colby, F/Lt, 101, 106
Collinson, Sgt, 29
Conrad, Edwin, 3
Cooper, F/Lt, 109
Coxall, W/O, 112
Cubitt, S/Ldr, 12

Davis, F/Lt 'Dizzie', 100, 111
Daniel, Col. James.L., 26
Dean, Gp/Capt 'Dixie', 67, 124
Drake, F/O, 110, 112

Edwards, Alan, 22

Farfan, F/O, 127
Foggo, W/O, 128

Gay, Lt Alex, 18, 19
Gee, F/Lt, 127
Gillespie, F/Sgt, 109
Gould, P/O, 95
Gould, Ron, 140
Grasser, Sgt, 12

Harris, F/O, 110, 118
Hart, Sgt Chris, 93, 94, 95, 96, 97, 99, 100,
    101, 103, 104, 105, 106, 107 108, 109,

110, 111, 116, 117.118, 119, 120, 121, 122, 127, 128, 133
Hawley, F/Lt, 114, 118
Hawthorne, F/Lt, 119, 120
Hay, Sgt, 36
Heitman, F/O Allan, 95
Herbert, P/O, 20
Hole, S/Ldr, 38
Honey, Gerry, 149
Houghton, F/O, 116
Howell, F/O, 110, 115

Irwin, F/Lt, 113

Jinks, F/Lt Bill, 115, 116
Johnston, P, 18

Larabee, Cpt, 25
Latus, Jack, 6
Latus, Joe, 6
Lee, F/O, 126
Lewis, Sgt, 127
Liebler, Wolfgang, 150
Lloyd, AVM Hugh Pughe, 101

Mahaddie, W/Co Hamish, 113
March, F/Lt, 38
Martens, Cpt Robert, 19, 23
Martin, F/O, 102
Mather, Gerry (uncle), 4
Mather, Gladys (aunt), 4
Mather, Gwen (cousin), 4
McAfee, Robert, 145
Mercer, Harald, 4, 68
Mercer, Richard, 4, 15

Neal, F/O , 128
Newton, Sgt, 121
Nelson, Cadet Ray. H, 143

Osborne, P/O, 44
O'Shea, Sgt, 103

Page, Mr, 5
Parsons, F.A, 25
Penfold, Sgt, 10
Platten, Tony, 7

Plumb, Don, 7
Pollock, Preston, 2
Price, F/O, 102, 103

Ralston, S/Ldr Roy, 82
Richard, Sgt, 101
Richardson, F/O, 114, 118
Robb, F/O, 126
Rodley, W/Cdr Ernest, 98
Roe, F/Sgt, 36
Ross, F/Lt, 115
Rowe, F/O, 121

Sather, Cpt, 22
Schmidt, Pat, 3
Searby, Diana, 140
Searby, John, 140
Shaw, Martin, 150
Shaw, Vicky, 150
Simpson, Major Charles. G., 25, 26
Soldano, Paul, 15, 16, 17, 18
Spinks, Sgt Derek, 133, 134, 135, 136
Stanhope, Lt Harold, 20
Stegman, F/Sgt, 116
Stevens, S/Ldr, 131

Temple, Reggie, 4
Theophilus, Sgt, 38
Thompsom, F/O, 113
Tindale, Ivy, 2
Topley, P/O Reg, 107
Turner, Cpl, 126
Tyrrell, Lt, 23

Vaughan, F/Lt, 30, 31
Vere, F/O R.H.M 'Percy', 135

Walker, Jean, 2
Watson, F/O, 136
Watson , P/O, 11
Weaver, Lt, 25
Whitehead, F/Sgt, 32
Woodall, P/O, 31
Wyman, Lt, 25
Wynes, F/O, 110, 118

Young, S/Ldr, 60